Getting the Best from

RATIO PLASTIC MODELS

By
Andy Farquarson

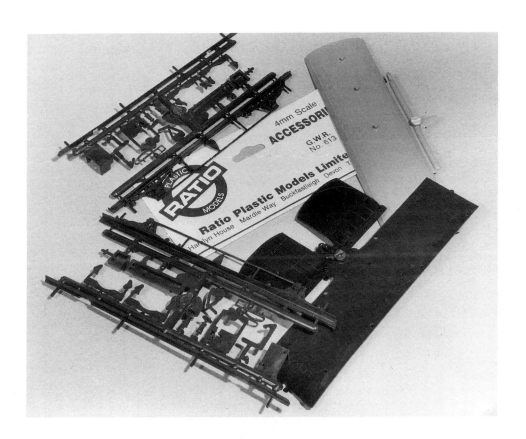

IRWELL
PRESS ▰▰▰

Copyright Irwell Press and Andy Farquarson, 1996
ISBN 1-871608-70-8

Dedication

To Eric, who obviously thought it worth that hundred quid.

Acknowledgements

I am greatly indebted to Mike Romans for his expert coverage of Ratio's signal range.

My thanks also to Roger Webster and Steve Taylor at Ratio Plastic Models; Tony Wright for photographs and advice; George and Chris; Michael Pritchard and PECO; Eileen of Eileen's Emporium; David White and Jaqui Statham at Slaters; my fellow members of Warley Model Railway Club; and all those authors whose published work has aided my research.

Finally, a special 'Thank you' to my wife, Sonja for proof-reading and putting up with it all and to Mr Nibbins for dragging me from the computer at meal times

Uncredited model photographs were taken by the author and prototype photographs are from the Irwell Press collection, copyright of the author and Irwell Press respectively. Other photographs are credited to the individual photographers, who hold the copyrights.

First Published in the United Kingdom by
IRWELL PRESS 1996
P O Box 1260, Caernarfon, Gwynedd, LL55 3ZD
Printed in Huddersfield by The Amadeus Press

CONTENTS

Preface

Modelling hobbies continue to grow in popularity. They appeal to people of all ages from all walks of life. Enthusiasts make models of almost anything that can be reproduced in miniature – aeroplanes, ships, spacecraft, dolls houses, theatres, military figures, cars and lorries.

Railways, in particular, have long proved an irresistible subject for modellers. Today, the railway modelling hobby encompasses a very wide range of techniques and specialisms. A typical layout will include landscape, architecture and railway infrastructure as well as the trains themselves. It will attempt to paint a portrait of the real world, past or present. The railway modeller has to be creative, resourceful and observant if that portrait is to convince viewers that they are looking at a slice of reality reduced in scale.

Because of its complexity, building a working model railway layout takes time. And, in our modern world, time for hobbies has to compete with time for work, time with the family and time at the supermarket. If everything on a layout had to be built from scratch, few layouts would get past the drawing board. So modellers welcome effective time-saving shortcuts, providing these don't compromise the finished result or the pleasure gained in achieving it. This is where the kit comes in.

Kits save the modeller the time-consuming task of gathering the raw materials and preparing them. Constructing a well designed kit can be as rewarding and satisfying as working from scratch and the result will often be as good, if not better, than a one-off handbuilt model.

Since the war, model railway kits have been produced in a wide variety of materials including wood, card, and cast or sheet metal. But the most common medium nowadays – and the one most suited to mass production – is plastic.

Ratio Plastic Models Ltd has been at the forefront of the hobby's plastic revolution for nearly forty years. A long-established family business, Ratio is now one of the UK's biggest independent producers of plastic kits for railway modellers. Its range, probably the most comprehensive on the market, covers most of the elements that make up a model railway layout – scenic items, lineside features, architectural structures large and small, signals, signal boxes, wagons, vans, and carriages.

This book is intended to help modellers get the best from this cornucopia and I have written it with the comparative newcomer in mind. All too often, it seems to me, authors imagine that all their readers will already have a well equipped toolbox, be familiar with modelling techniques and understand terminology that is often far from self-explanatory.

I have also assumed that not all readers are familiar with the whole Ratio range. In my view, getting the best from Ratio Plastic Models includes knowing what is available, especially the individual mouldings which can enhance and detail an 'out-of-the-box' model or aid kitbashing, crosskitting and scratchbuilding. So, at appropriate places in the text, I have included the kits' reference numbers – shown thus **[203]** – and there are complete product lists in the appendices.

Excellent though Ratio's kits are, the injection moulding process imposes certain limitations. If modellers understand these constraints, they will be better placed to enhance, refine and personalise the factory-fresh components and build more convincing and individual models from them. So I have briefly described how

One of my early shots at a Ratio 4mm scale van. This one is kit [566], the 'Mogo' motor car van.

the mouldings are produced, conveying, I hope, something of the Ratio team's enthusiasm and commitment to quality.

It is obviously not possible to describe every Ratio kit within 72 pages. So I have concentrated on those principles and techniques which can be applied across the whole range. The application of these general points to specific models is illustrated through a small selection of worked examples. I only wish there had been space for more, as building and photographing them was the most enjoyable aspect of producing this book.

To some extent, I have focused on the smaller, more mundane lineside items. This is because they are so often neglected. Modellers will often spend a lot of time on getting larger, more 'glamorous' models right – an engine shed or station building, for instance – while taking things like lamp posts or lineside huts for granted. A model railway, though dominated by the buildings, trackwork, locomotives and trains, will lack atmosphere and authenticity if no thought has gone into fencing, gates, telegraph poles, and other small details.

A large part of Ratio's output is 4mm scale but the techniques and the approach described in these pages are equally applicable to the 2mm and 7mm scale products. However, the Builder Pack series of architectural surfaces and accessories in 2mm scale are aimed at the scratchbuilder and so fall outside the remit of this book. Nonetheless, the Builders Packs are described in Appendix 3.

I have not included a separate chapter on Ratio's rolling stock kits (although they are covered in Appendix 2) for two reasons. Firstly, Ratio plans changes in this area so anything written in 1996 may soon be out of date. More importantly, kitbuilt rolling stock has either already been covered by a *Modelling Railways Illustrated Handbook* or is about to be. Constructing and improving wagon kits is the subject of *Getting the Best from Plastic Wagon Kits*, and a volume on carriage construction is in the final stages of preparation. There seems little point in covering the same ground as the earlier handbook or pre-empting the next one.

Mike Romans, a professional railwayman and signalling expert, has kindly contributed the chapter on Ratio signals. Railway signalling is a complex subject which deserves a book to itself so Mike is writing a *Modelling Railways Illustrated Handbook* on signalling which will be published soon.

In the following pages, you will find frequent exhortations to observe the prototype and to seek information and inspiration from the photographs published in railway books and magazines. I cannot stress the importance of going back to the prototype too strongly. A copy of a model you've seen on someone else's layout will rarely be convincing.

I built my first Ratio kit over twenty years ago. Since then, Ratio products have given me a great deal of pleasure for a very modest outlay. I hope that *Getting the Best from Ratio Plastic Models* will help you derive the same enjoyment and satisfaction from the range.

Finally, there is a saying that to borrow from one book is plagiarism but to borrow from many is research. I am happy to acknowledge my debt to published sources. I have also drawn on the expertise and experience of modelling friends in clubrooms and exhibitions up and down the country. So to everyone who has contributed to this book, however unwittingly, many thanks.

Andy Farquarson

A scene on Andy Calvert's N gauge layout *Nether Stowey*, now the centrepiece of Ratio's factory shop.

Chapter One
THE PLASTIC KIT

Injection moulded plastics have made a tremendous impact on modelling hobbies in general and on kits in particular.

In the model railway field, plastic kits are widely available and relatively inexpensive to buy. Although some are fairly complex and a few are very fiddly to put together, most are simplicity itself to build.

This user-friendliness stems partly from familiarity (most modellers under the age of fifty probably built Airfix aeroplanes when they were youngsters) and partly from the fact that no specialist tools, equipment or skills are needed for assembly.

The plastic medium (usually polystyrene) is neither brittle nor too soft. It is very easy to cut and work and, in the injection moulding process, can reproduce very fine detail and texture. It takes enamel paint well without the need for special preparation or priming.

No wonder the plastic kit has revolutionised railway modelling. Today, there can be few layouts which do not boast at least a couple of wagons and several lineside items built from plastic kits. And the chances are that the kit will be from the extensive range produced by Ratio Plastic Models Ltd.

The old firm

There are two remarkable things about the small South Devon town of Buckfastleigh. Firstly, there are thirteen letters in its name, all different, making it the longest place name in England without any repeated letters. Secondly, it is home to Ratio Plastic Models Ltd, one of the UK's most respected model railway manufacturing companies.

Ratio is one of the pioneering names in the history of the injection moulded plastic model railway kit. In the beginning (which in plastic kit terms means the early 1960s) the household names were Airfix and Kitmaster. But Ratio had

beaten them both to it, the firm's Iron Mink van kit appearing nearly a year before Airfix's inaugural wagon kit.

These early Ratio plastic kits (there were coke and iron ore hopper wagons as well as the Mink) were produced on a small hand-operated moulding machine. The moulds themselves (usually called 'mould tools' or just 'tools') were made using fairly unsophisticated workshop machinery from brass rather than steel. It was quite a contrast to Airfix's far larger operation.

Jack and Deva Webster had started the business in 1950 as Ratio Scale Models – no 'Plastic' in the name then. The first kits were made of wood and, for their time, made up into very good models if the builder took pains over their construction. The business was originally based in Chorley Wood near London and it was from there that the first Ratio plastic kit emerged in 1959.

Today, the business is run by Roger Webster, the genial son of the firm's founders. Roger is steeped in railway – and model railway – tradition. He worked for the Western Region's operating department at Paddington for many years, leav-

The home of Ratio Plastic Models Limited.

ing BR in 1969 to take up the post of Traffic Superintendent on the Isle of Man Railway.

In 1975 Roger left the Isle of Man to take over the helm at Ratio, following the death of his father. By this time, the business had moved to Sturminster Newton. The final move came ten years ago when Ratio took over the top floor of a converted wool mill in Buckfastleigh.

Nowadays, of course, Ratio relies on much more sophisticated technology than that early manual machine with its brass moulds. The firm has become a far bigger player and the product range has expanded enormously. Yet it retains the friendliness and commitment to quality of a small family concern, despite being one of the UK's largest manufacturers of model railway plastic kits.

When you consider the size of the range and the volume of the business, it comes as a surprise to learn that Roger has only five staff. Between them, they design, manufacture, pack and dispatch more than a hundred 4mm scale kits and over thirty in 2mm scale. And that's only half of it – there are at least as many accessory and materials packs as well. This product range breaks down fairly neatly into the following categories:

2mm scale lineside kits. These complete kits range in size and complexity from fencing and lamp posts up to an engine shed, GWR and Midland Rly signal boxes and a station building.

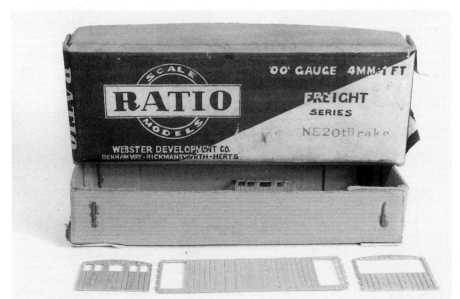

An early Ratio wood brake van kit.

A few of the kits in Ratio's extensive range.

2mm scale signals. A small range, mostly based on GWR prototypes.

2mm scale Builders Packs. Aimed at kitbashers and scratchbuilders, this is a series of moulded architectural surface sheets, augmented by various fittings.

4mm scale lineside kits. This is the real meat of Ratio's range. Over sixty kits, covering everything from telegraph poles to oil depots, weighbridges to water towers, goods sheds to grounded carriages.

4mm scale signals. Over twenty-five kits, some partly pre-assembled, covering GWR, LMS, SR and LNER types.

4mm scale rolling stock. Twenty wagon and van kits covering GWR, LMS, and SR prototypes and 14 carriage kits, mostly from the LMS and its constituents.

Components and accessories. These include items like window mouldings and buffer heads, wagon and carriage underframes and bogies, wheelsets and other accessories. Additionally, virtually all the individual mouldings from the kits are available separately.

7mm scale kits. A small range so far, but set to expand, it includes GWR square post signals, telegraph poles and SR concrete panel fencing.

Factory visits

The friendly atmosphere is the first thing you notice if you call at Ratio's Buckfastleigh HQ. Factory visitors are always very welcome, as Roger likes to meet his customers to discuss their ideas for new kits or possible improvements to the existing range.

It's always best to telephone first, though, if only to get directions. Buckfastleigh is on the A38 trunk road, about halfway between Plymouth and Exeter. Mardle Way is on the northern outskirts of the town and you can hardly miss Hamlyn House itself – it is the big, imposing stone building at the end of the street.

You take a lift up to the top floor and emerge into the shop. All the kits are on

sale, although occasionally one or two may be out of stock. Most of them are on show as well, fully constructed and painted. They are displayed in a series of beautifully modelled dioramas, the handiwork of Ratio's kit designer and works manager, Steve Taylor.

The centrepiece of the shop display is the large 2mm scale layout, *Nether Stowey*. Built to British N gauge standards by Andy Calvert, this prize winning layout has appeared at many exhibitions and has been featured in several modelling magazines. It includes many items from the Ratio range, the most impressive being a large mill building constructed from several engine shed kits.

The factory shop – visitors are always welcome.

As well as the complete kits, you can buy any single moulding from the factory shop. With over one thousand to choose from, it's only really practical to offer this service to personal callers, although Ratio will also supply mouldings by post providing you know which one you want. Roger also sells a limited selection of mouldings on the sales stand which he takes to many of the larger model railway exhibitions.

Behind the factory shop is the little studio where Steve Taylor designs and builds the kits, a cosy and intimate little corner nestling under the massive roof beams. By contrast, the toolmaker's machine shop is clinically clean and brightly lit. Towards the back of the factory, rows and rows of shelving hold boxes of kit components and beyond sit the two massive automated moulding machines. It's a fascinating place and well worth a visit if you're in the West Country.

Producing Ratio Kits

The process starts with design. This is not as straightforward as it might seem because a kit designer has to balance three often-conflicting factors.

First comes fidelity to the prototype. This involves hours of research, collecting any necessary drawings and reference works, studying as many photographs as possible and, quite often, site visits to measure the prototype. Armed with this information, the designer can produce a set of working drawings for the model and, in many cases, various mock-ups. There is an element of compromise here; it's no good ensuring that a particular component is an exactly scaled replica of the real thing if that makes it impractical to manufacture, too fiddly to assemble or too flimsy to be used on a layout. The second factor is the practicality of actually moulding the components. Some shapes are far harder than others to extract from the mould tool, for instance. To some extent, this factor also governs how far the complete model needs to be broken down into individual components at the design stage.

The designer must be fully conversant with the technical limitations of injection moulding and must also keep production costs in mind. Thoughtful arrangement of the components on their sprues can reduce the number of mouldings needed for a kit, saving machine time, simplifying packing and cutting down the amount of styrene wasted. The customer is the beneficiary; lower production costs mean cheaper kits.

The third design consideration is the user-friendliness of the finished kit. It must go together easily yet still provide challenge, satisfaction and value for money. The components must be an accurate fit, edges sharp and mating faces true, and feeds and runners must be arranged to help, rather than hinder, the builder.

So the designer of a plastic kit needs to be part railway enthusiast, part technician and part modeller. It's a hard row to furrow.

The mould tools

Once the design work is complete, the actual moulds, called 'tools', must be made, a process calling for great precision and some very sophisticated machinery.

Each individual moulding needs its own tool, so a kit containing more than one sprue will need several. The tool consists of two pieces, each made from a hefty solid steel blank. The shape of the finished model is cut from the two mating faces. When both pieces are placed on the moulding machine and brought together, they enclose the cavity into which molten plastic is injected to make the component. The tool is then parted and the moulded com-

ponent is pushed out. The two pieces of the tool must be very accurately united otherwise a step (called a 'part line') will be formed at the point where they part. So the tool incorporates a series of alignment dowels to ensure perfect register.

Because the moulding process is very temperature sensitive, the tool must not be allowed to get too hot. While it is on the moulding machine, a constantly monitored flow of liquid coolant is circulated around passages cut through the tool.

The finished plastic moulding is usually reluctant to leave the tool and must be forcibly extracted. Component design helps here, as some shapes are more difficult to extract than others; slightly tapering an edge can make a world of difference, for instance.

An elaborate system of hydraulically operated small rods, called 'pins', expel the moulding from the tool. As the plastic is still warm at this point, these extraction pins may mark the surface slightly. Again, good design can solve the problem. The point where the extraction pins bear on the component can be arranged so that any marks fall on the inside or underneath of the model. Sometimes, small removable protrusions (called 'pips') can be moulded onto the component for the pins to bear on.

This complex combination of registration, temperature control and extraction is common to all tools but it is the mould cavity itself that determines the shape, finish, level of detail and accuracy of a kit's components. It is the toolmaker's job to translate the designer's drawings and mock ups into highly accurate and perfectly finished cut-outs on the unforgiving steel surfaces of the tool.

Some of the work will be done using conventional machine shop equipment. A rectangular slot can be cut into the face of the mould tool with a milling machine to form part of the sprue. Similarly, a hole can be machine-drilled where a protruding extraction pip is required. But many of the shapes and textures of the finished component are far more complex than

Sophisticated equipment is called for to make the mould tools.

simple holes or slots. The fine detail is best produced by a process called spark erosion.

Spark erosion requires a complicated and very expensive computerised machine. In it, a copper electrode carrying a large electric current is advanced towards the face of the mould tool until it produces an electric arc. This is the 'spark' that eats away the steel. The whole operation takes place in an oil bath to carry away detritus and exclude contaminates.

The spark erosion machine doesn't substitute technology for the toolmakers' skill. Quite the reverse. Each copper electrode – and there may be several for a single component – has to be the exact shape of the required cavity and every one has to be individually made by the toolmaker.

The moulding process

Virtually all Ratio kits are made of high impact polystyrene by the injection moulding process. There are a few exceptions. The 2mm scale lineside fencing and the signal operating levers are moulded from polypropylene and ABS respectively, and the sections of arced corrugated roof are made by vacuum forming.

Just as its name suggests, the injection moulding process consists of forcing molten plastic into the cavity of the tool. This is done on another costly and sophisticated piece of equipment, a moulding machine. Ratio has two of these.

The raw material comes in the form of colourless translucent styrene granules. Before these are fed into the machine, special dyes (supplied as powder or granules) can be added so that the moulding comes out in the appropriate colour. An obvious example is the use of a browny-red dye for a component representing brickwork.

The Ratio Midland Rly signal box shows how the dyes can be used, with careful planning, to produce a pre-coloured kit.

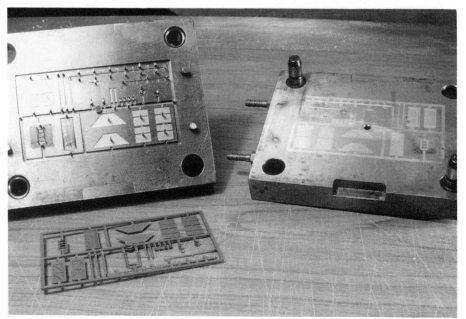

A typical mould tool and the component it produces.

One of Ratio's two moulding machines.

In fact, this model can be left unpainted, provided you can live with the slight sheen of the plastic surface.

The dye and plastic granules are heated in the moulding machine until they melt. The temperature is critical to ensuring just the right degree of viscosity. In most cases it will be around 180°C. The molten plastic is then injected under high pressure into the mould tool.

The two pieces of the tool must be very securely united and their faces must mate perfectly because the plastic enters at a pressure of about 1,000psi. Even the tiniest imperfection will allow a wafer thin layer of plastic to squeeze out of the mould cavity between the faces of the tool and this will produce 'flash' around the finished component.

The coolant circulating through the tool keeps the steel at a low enough temperature to allow the plastic to solidify, which takes around five or six seconds. The two pieces of the tool are then drawn apart, the extraction pins advance and the moulding drops from the tool into a collecting hopper. Then the machine closes the tool again to repeat the operation.

The end result

Most of the larger kits consist of several separate mouldings, each produced from its own tool. These may vary in size, colour and the number of individual components on them but certain features are common to virtually all mouldings, regardless of which tool spawned them.

Most of them will be made up of several separate components supported on a framework of plastic called a sprue. This frame is usually either round, rectangular or octagonal in section. Although it usually describes just the actual framework, you may occasionally find the word sprue used to mean a complete moulding. A modeller might say, for instance, 'I need two more sprues of fencing' or 'there is only one window on this sprue'

The individual bits contained on the sprues, the ones you build the kit from, I describe as components, rather than

parts, throughout this book. This avoids confusion with the word 'part' when used as a verb and 'part' also refers to the point at which the halves of a tool separate. 'Part the part from the sprue, checking for part-lines' would hardly be the clearest of instructions.

I've already described why part-lines occur. It's virtually impossible to produce mouldings that don't bear some evidence, however inconspicuous, of the parting of the tool. Usually it's only a faint line but a tool that has been in service for many years may produce a definite step on a moulding's surface. Most tools are designed so that the part-line runs along an edge where it cannot be seen but this is not always possible, particularly with round components.

But back to the moulding itself. At intervals, the components will be supported on short sections of plastic projecting from the sprue. These sections are called run-

ners. The components will be united to the runners by thin webs of plastic or 'feeds'. A feed is usually the best place to cut when removing components for use. Ratio's mouldings are designed so that the feeds will be unobtrusive on a component and will make it easy to remove from the sprue.

The moulding will also bear evidence of its extraction from the tool. Some components have to be designed with an otherwise unwanted slight taper to facilitate removal and there may also be marks where the extraction pins have pressed against the still-soft plastic.

One way of avoiding extraction pin marks on the surface of a component is to provide somewhere else for the pins to push against. Obviously, the sprue and its runners are suitable candidates. Pips are another way of overcoming the problem. These are small projections moulded onto the component, usually along its edge. Because they are only connected by thin feeds, they are easy to remove. Sometimes the pips are moulded onto the component itself, rather than alongside it, and these can often be left where they are as they are almost always sited where they will be invisible on the finished model.

Overcoming the constraints

As you have read, not only does the manufacturing process impose limitations on what can be produced, it also dictates that components will need a little preparation and refinement by the modeller. These constraints are inevitable if production costs are to be kept low enough to ensure the kits are reasonably cheap to buy.

Once you understand the limitations, you can work within them. And by knowing what to look out for, you will be better able to remedy any shortcomings of the injection moulding process. It's only when you ignore the realities of the plastic kit business that you end up disappointed. Here's a little story to illustrate what I mean.

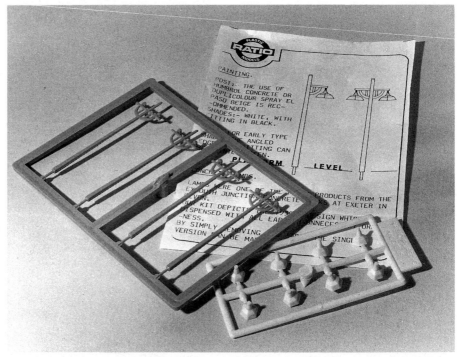

Components on their sprues. Photo: Tony Wright

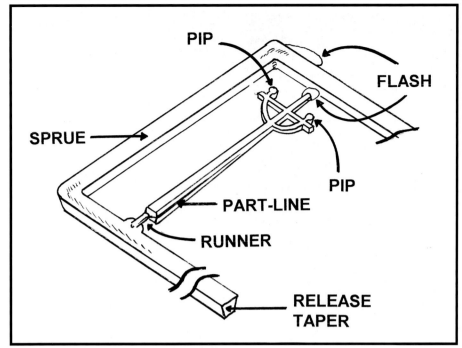

When Ratio introduced the 2mm scale engine shed kit, it received rave reviews. However, when the publisher of a self-styled 'finescale' modelling magazine saw a fully finished and painted display sample, he was less than impressed. This lofty chap examined the model closely for some minutes. Then he disdainfully declaimed 'The louvres on the roof ventilator are too thick' and stalked off, his nose in the air.

This little tale tells us more about his ignorance and elitism than it does about the Ratio engine shed. The practicalities of mass-producing quality models at a reasonable price (not to mention elementary good manners) are a closed book to people like that. They simply don't realise that a dead-scale plastic louvre would not only be almost impossible to manufacture in 2mm scale, but would be so flimsy that the modeller would hardly be able to use it.

So, given that some compromise is unavoidable, what effect does it have on how you set about building the kit? Well, you have to chop the components from the sprue yourself, for starters. The detail of how, and at what stage, it's best to do this is covered in Chapter 5.

Next, evidence of that bit of surgery will need burying. Usually this is simply a matter of rubbing down the remnants of the feeds, either with a piece of abrasive paper or on the sanding block described in Chapter 3. Occasionally another cut or a spot of paring will be necessary.

Moulding imperfections – things like extraction pin marks or part-lines – will need to be carefully scraped off or rubbed down. There may be flash to pare away with the scalpel or craft knife.

Mating faces of components, especially mitred corners, will need to be test fitted to ensure a perfect joint. Any imperfections, such as tiny projections, can be tidied up on the sanding block. In fact, at this stage it is often a good idea to have a full dry run, as described later.

Some components will be slightly overscale in thickness (the louvres mentioned above, for instance) and this will be particularly noticeable along their edges. By carefully scraping with the scalpel, a visible edge can be tapered to give the impression that the component is thinner than it actually is. This improves the appearance of the model without unduly weakening it.

Moulded relief can often be sharpened up. The grooves between planks on a door can be deepened or the inside corners of windows squared off, for example. You may wish to add texture or enhance what is already there; examples include scratching wood grain on a telegraph pole, or representing damaged and pitted bricks on a wall.

Quite a few components will have been moulded with a release taper to facilitate their extraction from the mould. Usually the taper will be along an edge where it doesn't need attention, but in some cases it will need remedying. Window glazing bars and the rails of lineside fencing are two examples.

In conclusion, although Ratio's plastic kits are as good as the technology and the economics of the market allow, careful preparation and a little remedial fettling will allow you to get the best from them. Ratio has already done ninety-five per cent of the work – the last five per cent is described in the following pages.

Ratio on the road. The exhibition sales stand at Warley National Model Railway Exhibition. Photo: Paul A Deerhart

One of Steve Taylor's beautifully modelled display dioramas. Ratio products include the retaining wall, spear fencing, yard crane, stone built hut, water tower and the loading dock.

Chapter Two
BEFORE YOU START

Be prepared, as Baden Powell said. Before you start to build your Ratio kit, you'll need somewhere suitable to work, a surface to work on, some tools and a few materials. It will also help if you have a clear idea of what you want to end up with and how you're going to get to that result, an 'approach' if you like. I believe that to gain the most satisfaction from the hobby, one of the fundamentals of the approach should be to model from the prototype rather than simply assemble a kit (or any other model) as an end in itself.

In this chapter, I will attempt to outline a few of the things that contribute to an approach – forming a clear idea of the desired result, familiarising yourself with the kit, gathering the prototype references and so on. Acquiring the right tools, collecting any necessary materials and mastering a few simple techniques also come under the general heading of preliminaries and these all have their own chapters later.

But the first requirement before you start is to a suitable, well-lit working area and a good surface to work on.

A place to work
One of the great advantages of plastic kits is that, within reason, they can be assembled almost anywhere. The only absolute essentials are a surface to work on, good light and (when using liquid adhesives) good ventilation.

Models can be (and often are) made in the most unlikely places. I have read about a commander of a nuclear submarine who, despite the cramped conditions, finds space to pursue his hobby. Another chap takes a large margarine tub to work every day containing a selection of tools, materials and components so that he can spend his summer lunch breaks modelling on a bench in a park near his office.

For some years, I lived on a canal boat with a cabin less than eight feet long (and three feet of that was the bed). Yet despite the small space and lack of mains electricity, I assembled quite a few Ratio plastic kits (a couple of which are illustrated in this book). And one of the most talented members of the Pendon Museum team turned out exquisite card buildings in his tiny caravan at the boatyard; he had electricity but hardly any more space than my boat cabin.

You probably won't be subject to such privations. You may even be able to arrange a permanent workshop in the utility room, the garage or the spare bedroom. Or you might be lucky enough to have a purpose-built shed in the garden.

However large or small, there are advantages in having a dedicated modelling place. Everything will be to hand and you won't have to pack things away after each session, for a start.

Against this, you will be cut off from the rest of the family and you may incur extra lighting and heating expenses. So

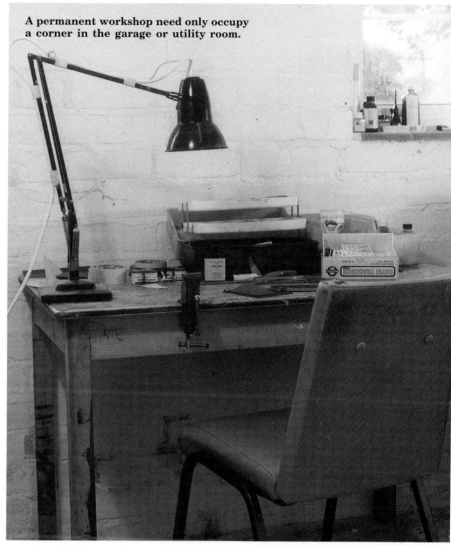

A permanent workshop need only occupy a corner in the garage or utility room.

even if you have a workshop, you may prefer to do some of your modelling in the living room. It will be more sociable, there'll be an extra pair of hands to call on if need be, you won't miss your favourite television programme and you will usually be warmer. Modelling in the house shouldn't be a problem because assembling a Ratio kit is a clean procedure, although there may be a few plastic slivers and shavings to sweep up. But you'll have to be careful with the liquid adhesive, especially if you've got kids. Most brands are flammable and they all give off vapour. The odour and toxicity of the fumes varies from one brand to another. The

Modelling at the dining table. An offcut of blockboard provides a good working surface and an anglepoise augments the ceiling lamp.

Simpler modelling tasks can be done on a tray or board on your knee. Ideal if you want to sit with the family.

golden rules are to ensure adequate ventilation (which may be a problem in the winter), to keep the adhesive away from sources of ignition and to guard against spillage. There is more on these adhesives in Chapter 4.

The most obvious places to work are on the dining table or the kitchen worktop. Either way, you will need good lighting (see below), a comfortable chair or stool and protection for the furniture. This last point is important. You cannot reasonably expect to use sharp knives, files, abrasives and adhesives directly on a table or a kitchen surface and remain on good terms with other people in the house.

So you need a surface to work on, firm, large enough and reasonably light. This need not be expensive. Many joinery works, shopfitters or furniture factories sell offcuts of suitable board and you can always look in skips or visit the civic amenity tip. Some DIY shops and furniture stores sell shop-soiled kitchen unit doors and similar items very cheaply and these can be used to work on.

Suitable materials for a work surface include medium density fibreboard, veneer-faced blockboard, melamine-faced chipboard and plywood. I use Contiboard, a relatively light chipboard with a hard, white melamine-type surface. It is widely available from DIY outlets and is fairly inexpensive.

Whatever you choose, the board needs to be thick enough to retain a flat, stable surface. Something around 15mm-30mm is about right, depending on the material. Formica, vinyl and melamine faced boards are slippery so glue pads of sponge or inner-tube rubber on the underside to stop them sliding around and to protect

the table top. I usually put a generous pad of newspaper under my workboard to protect the table.

The size of the work surface is up to you but anything less than eighteen inches square will probably prove too small.

Some simpler modelling tasks, such as refining and preparing the plastic components, can be done with the work board resting on your knees. This is a good way of working if you want to watch the television or sit in the garden. I use a cheap pressed wooden tea tray or a small offcut of lightweight blockboard in this situation. Obviously, you shouldn't do any heavier cutting on your tray – if the knife slips, your thigh will stop it. Similarly, an open bottle of liquid adhesive balanced on your knees is just asking for trouble. Another drawback of working on a tray like this is that you are likely to be hunched over which will make your back ache. Make sure you're comfortable wherever you work. Railway modelling is meant to be a hobby, not a penance.

Lighting

Wherever you work, good lighting is absolutely essential. Even if you have a well lit purpose-built workshop, additional localised lighting will make modelling easier. My own workshop has two 6ft fluorescent tube lights, augmented by the light from the windows, but I still need an anglepoise lamp over the work bench.

The anglepoise is probably the most suitable type of lamp for modellers. You don't need a smart new one; second hand anglepoises can often be picked up at junk shops, charity shops, markets or furniture auctions. As with any other second hand electrical goods, inspect the lamp before you buy it. Make sure the power cord is undamaged, the connections are sound and, in the case of a metal-framed lamp, that it is earthed.

Given a choice, go for the bayonet type of bulb holder rather than the screw fitting; bayonet bulbs are far more widely available and, usually, cheaper. For most situations, a 60W bulb is fine; 100W obviously gives more light but make sure that the lampholder and shade are suitable. A 100W bulb generates a lot of heat and some cheaper desk lamps should not be used with bulbs above 60W. If you are

modelling in a workshop, a corner of the garage or a dedicated room in the house, you can increase the light level substantially by painting the walls and ceiling white. Many garages have bare brick walls and a coat of white emulsion makes a really dramatic difference to light levels. You get more light from the same wattage so you'll save money and energy.

If you're working in the house, extra light will be a must. The normal, shaded pendant lamp in the middle of the ceiling probably won't be bright enough and your work will be in the shadow of your hands. You can see a couple of solutions in the photographs – a small standard lamp with a spotlight bulb, an anglepoise type of standard lamp, and a classic anglepoise desk lamp. There are plenty of other candidates.

Don't forget daylight. If you can work near to (and preferably facing) a window, you'll need less artificial light. Arrange your workshop so that the table or bench is by the window. In the house, move the table or your chair to take advantage of natural light.

With a comfortable, well lit place to work sorted out, it's time to think about exploiting the full potential of your kit.

Approach

Getting the best from a Ratio kit means more than simply opening the pack and following the instructions. To produce a really satisfying and realistic model, you should first have a clear idea of the result you want and how you are going to get it.

Firstly, you want your kit to be realistic; that is, to present a convincing impression of the real thing. Ratio has made a major contribution at the design stage by ensuring that the kit is dimensionally accurate and to scale. Most of the models are drawn from original plans and diagrams, augmented by field trips to photograph and measure the prototype wherever possible.

But a realistic finished model still depends on you. It demands careful construction and eradication of the compromises inherent in mass production and the manufacturing process. It relies on skilful, observant painting and finishing. The kits can't cater for all the possible variations nor incorporate all the details that differentiated, say, one Midland Rly signal box from another or all the variants in a train of clay wagons. There is plenty of room for your own researches here.

Second, you want your kit to stand out from the crowd. You don't want just another Ratio engine shed – you want a model with a spark of individuality, a model that says 'I made this'. Expressed another way, if you fancy a grounded carriage body on your layout, would you prefer one based on an actual prototype, one that *you* built using the Ratio kit as a starting point, rather than the same Ratio grounded carriage body kit found on every other layout?

Slavishly following the picture on the packet will simply result in a clone of every other model built from that particular kit. So will copying something you've seen on

Ratio designers take great pains to ensure the accuracy of the kits. This often involves field research; here is the prototype of the GWR signal box kit [500], photographed at Highley on the preserved Severn Valley Railway.

someone else's layout, at the club or at an exhibition. In both cases you will have made a model of a model, rather than one of a real wagon, building or whatever.

Realism

A model railway layout, taken as a whole, can be viewed in two ways. Firstly, it is an operational system on which trains can be run, hopefully in a prototypical manner. It is also (or, at least, it *can* be) a scenic model, a small section of the real world as seen from a distance. As such, it is more than just a model *railway*, it is a model of a scene with a railway in it. The scenic side includes not only all the buildings and other man made structures but the colour, texture and shape of the landscape itself.

To be convincing, the layout must be a unity rather than a collection of disparate constituents. All the things that contribute to the scene – track, trains, buildings, ground textures, foliage and so on – must be consistent. There are two important considerations here. First, there should be broadly the same degree of detail in all the elements. Second, their texture, tone and colour should be consistent and harmonious.

For example, take two simple open goods wagons, one built from a Ratio kit and one from a ready-to-run (RTR) range. Even if you ignore the important matter of prototype conformity (the RTR underframe will probably be a compromise design, intended to fit under any similar wagon body in the range, whereas the kit's running gear will be an accurate representation of the correct pattern), there will be a considerable disparity in the level of detail. That on the kit will not only be finer, there'll be a lot more of more of it.

When it comes to finish, the two wagons will clash as well, assuming you paint and weather the kit along the lines described elsewhere. The RTR wagon will be not only be brighter and shinier but its printed lettering will look very different to the transfers on the kit. If you marshal these two wagons in the same train on your layout, any illusion of reality will be dashed by their inconsistency.

Of course, that is not to say that RTR wagons can't be used alongside kit built ones. By toning down their factory finish, weathering them and improving or substituting their running gear, you can end up with a superb model. This sort of work is described in *Detailing and Improving Ready to Run Wagons*, a sister volume in this series.

This need for consistency applies as much, if not more, to structures and buildings as to wagons and other purely railway items. Compare, say, one of the old fashioned pre-printed card kits for buildings with an equivalent moulded plastic offering (I'm not talking about the latest generation of specialised card kits, such as the superb offerings from firms like Freestone Model Accessories or Howard Scenics, but the popular sort still sold in most model and hobby shops). The biggest difference will be surface relief. Put simply, the card kit won't have any, at least as far as areas of brick, tile or slate are concerned. Again, the plastic kit will also benefit from more – and finer – detail, with moulded gutters, downpipes, doors and other features. The finish will differ, too; however it is painted, the plastic kit won't have the smooth, slight sheen of the printed card.

But no single model railway company makes everything – track, locos, rolling stock, buildings, structures, lineside details, ground textures, foliage – that is needed for a scenic layout. And, even if one did, all these things could not be made of the same stuff. Not even plastic is that versatile. To build a layout, you have to mix'n'match manufacturers and materials.

So how can you integrate all these separate elements into a harmonious whole? Putting the same amount of effort into each individual model is obviously important. It's no good laboriously adding every last detail to a building if the one next to it is completely plain and unadorned.

But uniformity of detailing is not enough on its own. The other important factors affecting homogeneity and cohesion (and, therefore, realism) are finish, colour, tone and weathering.

Gloss finish is the thing to avoid. In the real world, even a clean car looks less and less shiny the further away it is. And gloss paint on doors and windows has no more than a slight sheen when seen from a hundred yards. Brick walls, roofs, unpainted wood, grass, trees, pavements, earth – all these look absolutely matt in ordinary daylight.

When it comes to colour, the main thing is to keep it fairly muted. However strong the colour of something in the real world, it will appear weaker and flatter the further we move from it due to the effects of the atmosphere. Even though a layout may only be a couple of feet from the viewer, the scale equivalent viewpoint is

A photograph like is invaluable if you want to add interior detailing to Ratio's signal boxes. Railway magazines (such as *British Railways Illustrated*, *Bylines*, *Railway Magazine* and *Railway World*) are a good source and back issues can often be picked up cheaply.

much further away and our colours should enhance this impression of distance.

Similarly, the tonal value of all the models should be reasonably uniform. A strong, bright building will stand out from its fellows, compromising realism. Tonality can also help to exaggerate the illusion of depth in a scene; stronger tones and colours at the front, lighter tones and weaker colours towards the back.

Consistency of weathering is also necessary. If there are rain streaks on one structure, they should be on others as well (unless there's some obvious reason why not). The same applies to algae, mould, lichen and similar staining at the bottom of walls. Even little things like the direction of the imaginary sun should be considered; paint fades more on the sunny side of a fixed structure and more mould grows on the shaded side.

Getting to know the kit

Having got a kit home, it is very tempting to open the box, grab your tools and adhesive and get stuck in. Even though you're unfamiliar with the kit, the first stage may look obvious and if you've built a similar item from the range, you may think the procedure will be the same. But often neither assumption is true. As most experienced modellers will tell you, a little restraint at that exciting 'opening the box' stage will pay dividends later.

The most sensible approach (and the one that I now always adopt) is to get to know the kit before you start work. Use the written instructions and the exploded diagram to identify every component. Try to become really familiar with the kit. Ask yourself some questions: Has everything that should be included been packed? Where do all the bits go? What order of assembly does Ratio recommend? Can I improve on or adapt that order? Does the model break down into sub-assemblies? Which components will be more easily painted while they're still on the sprue?

If you intend to modify the kit or adapt it to your specific layout, now is the time to decide what needs doing, how it will be done and what (if any) additional components or materials you will need.

If anything is damaged or missing from the box (a very rare occurrence with Ratio's kits), take the kit back to your supplier, who should replace it there and then. Occasionally (if you've bought the kit at a model railway exhibition, for instance) that may not be possible. Write to Ratio, explaining the problem; they will usually send the missing item by post.

Back to the instructions. It is surprising how many people get into bother by ignoring or misunderstanding them. In my experience, the recommended assembly sequence is reliable if you are building the model as intended. Ratio staff build all the kits (both for pre-production proving and for photographic and display purposes) and the instructions are written during assembly so you're getting it straight from the horse's mouth.

Having studied the instructions, you may find it useful to jot your own notes on them. You can also do this during construction. Sometimes it will only be a tick as each stage is completed, sometimes a sentence or two to remind you that a detail will need adding later. If, like most people, you can only snatch the odd hour here and there for modelling, the kit may be left partly built for days or even weeks. You may find it easier to pick up the work later if you make a note of what you were about to do next.

Research

Research, in this context, doesn't mean sitting in libraries, poring over tedious and earnest railway histories or blueprints that haven't seen daylight since Queen Victoria was on the throne. The major resources for this sort of realistic modelling are photographs and on-the-spot observation. You can also join one of the more specialised study and research societies dedicated to various aspects of railway history.

Photographic research is one of the hobby's most pleasant aspects. There's nothing like curling up on the sofa to browse through a pile of books and magazines looking for pictures to inspire and inform your modelling.

There are plenty of specialist railway publishers. When it comes to illustrated books (and photographs are what we're looking for here), Irwell Press is well to the fore. Irwell's large format hardback *Annual* and *Summer Special* are particularly useful, profusely illustrated and good value for money.

Other photographic albums that are particularly useful include those from Middleton Press. Each album is devoted to a specific line or section and contains about 120 photographs with extended captions, brief histories, maps and diagrams. The series coverage is concentrated on south and south-west England. At the time of writing, the price is £10.95, but you can often pick up second hand copies cheaply at model railway exhibitions or the shops at preserved sites.

Bradford Barton produced dozens of photographic albums throughout the 1970s and '80s. Although these are now out of print, there were so many published that getting hold of them second hand is no problem. Until recently, they could be bought for a couple of quid but the prices are starting to creep up. Like the Middleton books, Bradford Barton's contain a hundred or so black and white pictures.

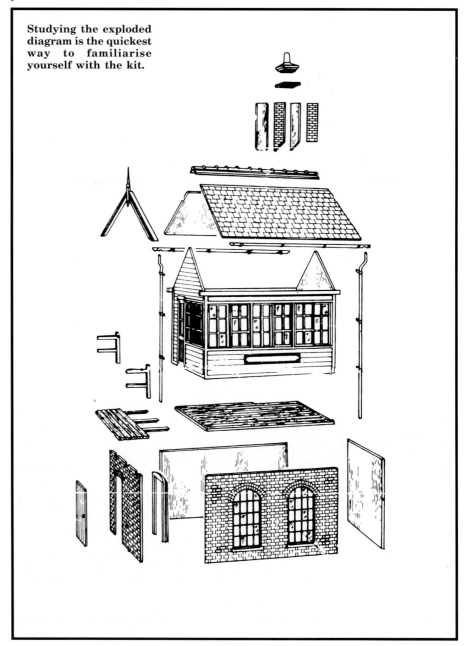

Studying the exploded diagram is the quickest way to familiarise yourself with the kit.

You can take your own photographs to help you model details accurately. These close-up pictures, both taken recently on the Severn Valley Railway, show signal box sliding windows - Ratio kits [223, 237, 500, 503 and 536] - and tank fittings on a water tower [230, 528].

Railway magazines are another good source of photographic reference. *British Railways Illustrated* from Irwell Press is the front runner for photographs of steam age subjects but there are plenty of other titles on the bookstalls. For modellers of the post-steam era and today's railway, *RAIL*, *Traction*, and *Modern Railways* all provide plenty of photographic material, much of it in colour. And, of course, model railway magazines often publish photographs of prototype subjects. Best in this regard is *Modelling Railways Illustrated*, parent to this book, which has a regular feature, Modelling Moment, devoted to modellogenic nooks and crannies of the real railway.

Again, the second hand market will enable you to build up a large collection without spending a fortune. Even the small-est local model railway exhibition will have a stall selling old magazines cheaply and many of the fund-raising shops run by preserved railways are packed to the gills with them. A carrier bag stuffed with back issues of *Steam World* for a quid is pretty cheap research by any standards.

Of course, you may wish to delve into the particular as well as soaking up the general and virtually every aspect of railways is catered to by a plethora of specialist societies. But only one, the Historical Model Railway Society, is dedicated (as its name suggests) to researching into and recording the history of Britain's railways with the modeller in mind.

The HMRS is custodian of several major photographic collections and many smaller ones, totalling over thirty thousand individual photographs. Prints are offered to members for their own use at a modest cost. There are also over five thousand individual drawings available to members and a huge library of books.

Members can also take advantage of the 'company steward' service. The stewards are experts on particular railway companies so if, for example, a member needed details of the lining applied to a Midland Rly clerestory carriage immediately after the Great War, he would turn to the relevant steward.

Transfers are another area where HMRS can supply modellers' needs. The Society is owner and sole supplier of the well-known Pressfix and Methfix ranges. You don't need to be a member to buy these, either by post or from selected model shops, although you will get a discount if you are.

Look out for the HMRS at many of the major model railway exhibitions. Their stand usually has several boxes of period photographs for sale. Contact details are in Appendix 1.

On the spot observation

I have already emphasised the importance of working from photographs and there's nothing to beat having a selection of colour prints propped up on the bench as *aides memoir* while you make a model. This is especially true during the painting and finishing stages. And if you've taken them yourself, so much the better.

Today, nearly everyone owns a camera and modern films give accurate colour rendition, are cheap to buy and can be processed almost anywhere. It has never been easier to record colour and build your models from a selection of your own pictures.

This visual 'research' is so enjoyable that it often becomes an end in itself. If you want a pictorial record from which to model a barn, wait for a sunny day, grab the camera, whistle the dog up and set off for a country walk. If you live in a town or city, make it a family day out. You can take the car or, better yet, go on the train. You'll not only get a breath of fresh air but you'll meet some interesting people and learn something new.

Urban railways offer even more potential and excitement to the observant. Not only can you record what you see but you have a custom-made excuse to chat to railway staff in their idle moments and learn a lot about the railway and its operation.

Of course, much has changed in recent years and a modern mainline with its continuous welded rail, steeply shouldered ballast, concrete sleepers and overhead electrification structures is a far cry from the fishplated, wooden sleepered, bullhead railed permanent way and telegraph poles of years gone by.

Much remains timeless, however, and awaits your lens. For instance, the subtlety of weathering effects on concrete, stone or brick; the way water seeps out of cutting sides; the siting and fencing of the boundary; the variety of grasses and weeds along the lineside (although the further back in time you go, the more frequently the lineside was cleared of undergrowth) and much more.

The permanent structures such as bridges, tunnel portals, viaducts, retaining walls, station platform faces and so on are often as they were thirty, fifty or more years ago. In many cases, so are other features. I'm looking at a picture of Lenham (near Ashford, Kent) as I write. A Eurostar is passing through the station but otherwise it looks pretty much as it has done since the war.

When buildings are taken out of railway use, they often remain much as they were. Trains may stop beside a station building that is now home to the local lorry operator, his fleet parked where the goods yard used to be. His mechanic may have appropriated the little office once occupied by the coal merchant and the goods shed will provide plenty of detail to record even though it's been colonised by jovial young tyre fitters who sing and dance the long hours away. 'You can't get better...'

Even when the railway itself has long gone, there is still much to see. Within a few miles of my village, I can study the faded traces of the original lettering on a Great Central goods shed, photograph the magnificent blue brick viaducts and bridges that characterised the GCR's London Extension, or imagine a 9F rattling an Annesley to Woodford freight through the lattice girder bridge that still spans the West Coast Main Line at Rugby. Then there's the more prosaic remnants of the Weedon-Leamington line, closed to traffic for over thirty years, less than a mile away from my home.

Preserved railways are another obvious destination for a field research trip. I doubt if many people in England live more than a couple of hours drive from one of them.

During school holidays and at weekends, you may find photographic access restricted for safety reasons but on weekdays and out of season, with no trains running, you will probably find you can wander around at will with your camera.

Some purists claim you should be cautious about treating preserved artefacts as accurate historical sources. The paint on the locomotives may not have been prepared from Swindon specifications to the exact shade of GWR green, they claim. Fair enough. But you can see, and record, the overall look of the steam age railway and the way it fitted into its environment.

The Midland Rly signal box [536] is one of Ratio's most recent 4mm scale kits. The components are pre-coloured (although the finished model will look even better if you paint and weather it) and the box can be shortened or extended to represent prototype variations. Quite a few of these boxes are still in service on former Midland lines.

Chapter Three
TOOLS

You don't need many tools to assemble a plastic kit. Some of those described below are essential, others will make things easier or speed the work up and a few are luxuries.

Very few modellers go out and buy a comprehensive tool kit at one go. Usually, they build up slowly, adding new tools as they find a need for them or as cash allows. This process often takes years.

For the benefit of newcomers, I've whittled the selection down to a minimum tool kit. This appears after the alphabetical listing. There's also a section on tool maintenance and safety.

You will find many of the tools in the list are easily available but others are harder to find. Modellers collect tools from many fields – engineering (vices, squares, and files for instance), the medical profession (scalpels, small forceps, dental burrs and the like) and the jewellery and watchmaking trades (tweezers, turnscrews, pin chucks and so on).

There are a number of specialist firms supplying tools for railway modellers. Some (among them Proops and Shesto) mainly cater to watchmakers and jewellers but also have a foot in the model railway camp. Other businesses (such as Eileen's Emporium and John K Flack) specialise in selling tools and materials to modellers. A selection of tool suppliers, most of which attend the larger exhibitions and supply the better model shops, appears in Appendix 1.

One piece of advice, often repeated but always worth another airing, is to buy the best quality tools you can afford and look after them (there are some notes on maintaining tools later on).

It's proved difficult to draw a rigid line between 'tools' and 'techniques'. Often the best way to describe a tool involves explaining what it is used for and how, so some overlap with Chapter 5 is inevitable.

CUTTING TOOLS

Surgical scalpel
Medical scalpels are specifically designed for precise, delicate work. This makes them ideal for modelling. I recommend the brass handled ones made by Swann Morton which take standard 'click-to-fit' surgical blades.

You can either buy medical blades in sealed sterile packs or cheaper, non-sterile, ones intended for craft work. The medical ones last longer and always seem sharper when new. Blades come in many shapes and sizes (trying to work out what surgeons do with each sort makes me squeamish) but for modelling work, I recommend only two. These are the 10A blade with its short, straight cutting edge and the longer, curved 10.

Don't let the blade become blunt. Change it frequently. To remove a blade for replacement, *don't* try to grip the old one between your fingers and pull it out –

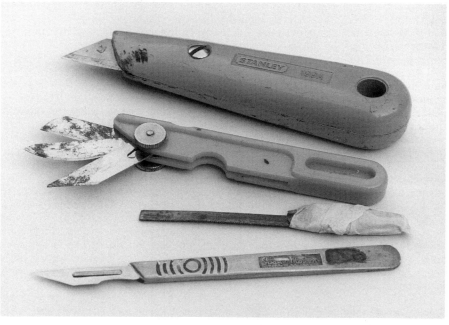

A selection of cutting tools. From the top: the traditional Stanley knife; the Unitool with straight, curved and angled blades; a length of hacksaw blade with one end bound in adhesive tape; and a Swann Morton surgical scalpel.

you'll soon find out how sharp it is. The best way is to stick a short length of masking tape along the blade and then, holding the handle in the normal way, press and twist the blade on a hard surface until it snaps. This should leave the two halves of the broken blade safely stuck to the tape. Put it straight into the dustbin.

To insert a new blade, carefully unwrap it and, holding it in a fold of stiff paper or card, ease its slot over the retainer on the handle until it is held lightly then, holding the tool in the normal way, press the tip of the blade against a firm surface until it 'clicks' home.

Scalpels and blades are available from any of the specialist tool suppliers listed in Appendix 1, from medical suppliers and from larger dispensing chemists.

Craft knives
For less delicate work, I use an ordinary modellers' craft knife. There is a wide variety of types widely available.

Swann Morton does a nice one and their No 2 blade is the most useful. This knife is sold in many model and craft shops and you can also buy it at the larger model railway exhibitions. Swann Morton also

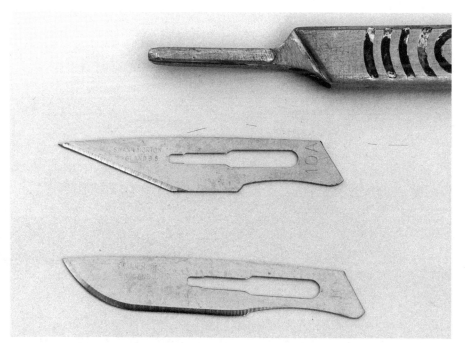

The scalpel handle with the two most useful shapes of blade. The angled 10A is used for straight cuts, the curved 10 for scraping and paring.

produces the Unitool. This has a sturdy plastic handle and three fold-out blades (curved, tapered and straight) which are locked in place by a knurled wheel.

X-acto is another well known hobby tool manufacturer, producing several useful craft knives. The range is sold in model and craft shops and at many model railway exhibitions as well as by specialist tool suppliers. The X210 and X211 blades are equivalent to 10 and 10A scalpel blades.

Most model and craft shops sell other plastic handled craft knives with various shapes of blade. Have a browse, but don't choose anything too flimsy.

Snap-knives (the sort where each short section of blade can be snapped off as it loses its edge and a new, sharp section advanced from the handle) are widely sold by DIY chains, hardware shops and some model shops. Obviously, you need to be careful not to snap the blade off as you are working and to be wary of putting much pressure on them. Some modellers swear by them, but I don't recommend this sort of knife.

Stanley knife
For heavier cutting, the good old traditional Stanley knife is hard to beat. You can buy one from most DIY chains, hardware stores and model shops. The cheaper imported look-alikes and DIY superstore own-brand handles are OK (and a little cheaper) but stick with pukka Stanley brand blades. They're made sharper, stay sharper and last longer. You can get variously shaped blades for these knives but for modelling the standard short straight sort is best.

There are two types of handle. The original pattern holds the blade on a location spigot cast into the handle itself, the other carries the blade on a retractable slide. I much prefer the non-retractable type. It's firmer and safer, in my view.

Stanley blades have the great advantage that they are easy to resharpen on an oilstone. If you're a woodworker, you'll probably already have a stone to sharpen your chisels and plane irons. If not, buy a combination stone (that is, one with a coarse face on one side and a smooth one on the other) from any DIY store for about a fiver. It's not only useful for resharpening Stanley blades, of course – it has a hundred and one workshop uses, such as turning old electrical screwdrivers into little scrapers and chisels. And, of course, you can whip the family carving knife over it.

Razor saw
A razor saw is very useful for making straight, accurate cuts through thicker material. Although you won't have much call for it if you're constructing the kit 'out of the box', it comes into its own once you start kitbashing. Modellers sometimes refer to this tool as an 'X-acto saw', so no prizes for guessing who makes most of them.

A razor saw looks like a miniature woodworkers' tenon saw and is used in much the same way. Because the blade is held rigid and straight, a razor saw is the best tool for making long straight cuts,

especially if the resulting edges will be butt jointed to another component.

A razor saw cut is about 0.5mm wide, so be sure to cut on the waste side. It is important that the work is well supported and held steady. Some sort of guide for the blade will be necessary to ensure accuracy and this is discussed in Chapter 5.

Xuron shears
This tool got rave reviews when it first appeared. The panegyrics are well deserved – the Xuron is magic. The American manufacturer describes the shear as a track cutter. It does that job excellently, but once you've got one, you'll find innumerable other uses for it. It is available by mail order from Proops or Eileen's Emporium (see Appendix 1) and many other model railway outlets.

The shear blades, which overlap slightly when they meet, are flat and ground on the inner face only. This means that you can cut off surface projections virtually flush. It's ideal for cutting plastic kit components from their sprue and for nipping off extraction pips.

You can chop up quite thick styrene with the Xuron as well. If you use it on plastic rod or strip (or, for that matter, brass or nickel sections) it will leave a clean, square end. Several Ratio kits contain etched brass components and the Xuron excels at neatly separating the individual components from the fret.

Look after it and it'll last a lifetime. Don't try to cut thick or hardened metal and keep the tool in the sturdy wallet it comes with.

Side cutters
These are useful but certainly not essential. I find them handy for chopping up sprues into manageable pieces and for releasing parts if the runner or feed is thick, saving the Xuron shear for finer work. Side cutters also have many other uses around the workshop and home.

Unless you intend to use them for precise or heavier work, the cheap sidecutters from the Far East which are sold on market stalls and in discount shops will be good enough. They only cost a couple of

pounds, but remember you get no more than you pay for.

Junior hacksaw
Not really an essential but it can sometimes get in where the razor saw can't reach and it will cut through thicker material more quickly.

OTHER TOOLS

Cutting mat
It is better to cut on a firm but yielding surface than directly onto a hard worktop or bench. The knife will be less likely to slip, skid or follow slits made in the surface by previous cuts when the blade breaks through the workpiece. You can use a sheet of thick card, throwing it away when it gets scored, but a much better option is a purpose-made cutting mat.

The mats most often used by modellers are made of a green dense rubbery material. They are marked with a grid to aid squareness and come in A2, A3, A4 and A5 sizes. Prices range from £2.50 for the A5 size to about a tenner for the A3. Knife cuts are self-healing and if the blade slips from the work, the mat will stop it before it ends up in your leg or hand.

You can buy cutting mats from art, model or craft shops and at model railway exhibitions. They are also available from specialist tool suppliers. One of the cheapest sources I've found is Freestone Model Accessories; their address is in Appendix 1.

Drills and bits
If you do a lot of modelling, you may already have a 12 volt minidrill. This is probably overkill. Under power, small drill bits will be very likely to bind in styrene or melt themselves through rather than cut.

It's so easy to drill through plastic that a hand-powered tool is much more suitable. You retain far more control, especially useful if the hole is to be blind.

There are various types of hand drills available from specialist tool suppliers and model shops. The most useful is the double-ended, knurled type with revers-

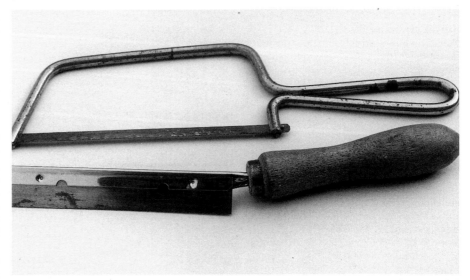

A Junior hacksaw, top, occasionally comes in handy but a razor saw is essential once you start modifying plastic components. The blade is fitted into a wooden file handle but X-acto sell a purpose-made saw handle.

The close-cutting precision Xuron shear on the left is a joy to work with. The cheap side cutter on the right has its uses as well.

ible colletts in each end to take any size drill bit up to one-eighth inch diameter. These are often described as pin vices or pin chucks.

An alternative is the Archimedean screw drill. You pop the drill bit in the chuck, press down lightly on the top thumbpad and work the collar up and down. It's good classical stuff – very Greek. And cheap.

You will also need a small selection of drill bits. The old imperial 'number series' are now much harder to come by (and more expensive) than the metric equivalents. I recommend the following sizes as a 'starter' selection: 0.5mm, 0.7mm, 0.9mm, 1.25mm.

Other useful sizes include 0.45mm to take the most popular size of straight brass wire (0.45mm or 26swg gauge); 0.52mm to take 20thou plastic Microrod; and a somewhat larger size (2mm or upwards) for countersinking or de-burring.

Fibreglass pencil or stick
These tools are widely used during construction of etched brass or cast whitemetal kits but you seldom see them mentioned as aids to modelling in plastic.

However, the propelling-pencil type of fibreglass burnishing tool has a couple of uses in this context. It is very effective at removing the rag or feathering which can result from scraping or filing, especially around window apertures. Another use is an abrasive. Used carefully, the fibreglass pencil removes the sheen from moulded surfaces without damaging detail. This leaves a dead matt finish which provides a better key for paint.

Files
Small needle files (often referred to as Swiss files) are useful for preparing and refining plastic components. However, it's not worth buying the best quality in this instance. Rather than genuine Swiss files, opt for the cheap wallets of half-a-dozen Chinese needle files which can be bought at tool sales, on market stalls, at model railway exhibitions or from the suppliers listed in Appendix 1.

The square, triangular and flat shapes are the most useful, especially for cleaning out and sharpening corners. However, filing styrene tends to bring up ragged feathering along edges. As this needs scraping away, I often prefer to use the scalpel or home-made chisel rather than the file to remove the material in the first place. Still, the small file has its place.

One problem with these fine files is that they very soon clog with plastic. A

once-over with a brass-bristled suede brush will clear the detritus.

You can also buy handles to hold most needle files from the specialist tool suppliers listed in Appendix 1. There's more on files and handles under the heading, 'maintaining tools' below.

Magnifiers
If you're doing a lot of fine detailing or your eyes are less than perfect, you may find a magnifier of some sort useful. These range from elaborate free-standing magnifying glasses with integral fluorescent lamps to simple eyeglasses, and the prices vary to match. If you visit photographic labs or suppliers, look out for those folding magnifiers that are used for viewing transparencies over a lightbox. The best bet is a cheap plastic jewellers' eyeglass – not essential, but very handy.

Paintbrush to apply liquid adhesive
Always discard the stubby little brush attached inside the screw cap which you'll get with some brands of liquid adhesive. You need something smaller and more subtle. An artists' brush, size 1 or 0, is big enough for most jobs. It needn't be a top quality brush but choose one with a good point. Obviously avoid any with plastic ferrules or handles.

I quite often recycle brushes that have been used for painting models. Once a brush has lost its fine point or the bristles have become distorted, it may not be good enough for detail painting but will still be useful as an adhesive brush. What's more, the action of the solvent will clean all traces of paint from it. This may give the brush an extra lease of life for painting.

While on the subject of brushes, here's a little dodge which professional signwriters use to restore the shape and point to brushes that have become 'bent' or ragged. Clean all the paint from the brush (liquid adhesive can help here, as noted above) then plunge the bristles, right

It's not worth spending a fortune on top quality Swiss needle files. A wallet of the cheap sort made in China will do for modelling in plastic. Beside the wallet is a riffler file, the curved ends of which allow you to rub the parts other files can't reach. At the right of the picture are two of the most useful shapes, triangular and rat-tail.

up to the ferrule, into boiling water. The water must be actually boiling and the brush must be withdrawn almost immediately. The bristles will straighten out and regain their set. It only works with 'natural' (as opposed to nylon or daylon) bristles held in metal ferrules, however.

Pencil

Nothing special here; just an ordinary HB grade for general marking out. Keep the pencil sharp (round pencils are easier to sharpen than the hexagonal ones) and for a really fine point, spin the graphite tip on a scrap of abrasive paper.

Plastic scriber or 'scrawker'

Not, as its name suggests, the precision pointed tool used by engineers to mark out metal workpieces. A 'scrawker' is a hooked tool that can be used to scribe swarf-free lines on plastic, either as an aid to snapping off sections or to represent planking, brickwork and so on. Some modellers fashion these from old lengths of hacksaw blade but Tamiya make a ready-to-use deluxe version, described as a Plastic Scriber. This is sold by many model and toy shops (including branches of the Beatties chain) and by some of the suppliers listed in Appendix 1. Useful but not essential.

Pliers

A good quality, medium sized pair of box pliers are useful for bending and shaping wire and metal. Smaller, snipe-nosed pliers with smooth jaws are handy for all sorts of gripping and bending jobs.

It's false economy to buy cheap pliers, so go for the best you can afford. The sort you find on market stalls are a waste of money. The specialist tool suppliers in Appendix 1 all supply a variety of shapes and sizes at reasonable prices.

Steel rule

This serves several functions. It can be used to measure or as a straightedge for marking-out and cutting. It can guide a scalpel or razor saw when you're cutting. The end can be used as a square.

A six-inch steel rule is most convenient for 2mm scale work and for smaller 4mm scale models but for longer items, such as platforms, canopies or valancing, the 12ins version is preferable. Buy both if you can afford them but if you have to choose, go for the smaller one first. Buy a good quality make such as Rathbone Chesterman.

Squares

Some modellers claim that they can assemble models perfectly square without the eponymous tool; but then how do they know their work *is* square? A square, in my view, is essential.

I have two on the bench when I'm assembling plastic kits. One is a small (about four inches long) standard engineers' square and the other a cheap triangular plastic square from a geometry set. Other aids to keeping things true include the end of the steel rule and various small wooden blocks.

Two steel rules and two squares. Of these, the small engineers' square is the most essential.

If you work on one of the purpose-made cutting mats or the assembly surface detailed below, the printed grid will help you set models up square in plan view. If you are working directly on a board, you can draw a grid of right angled lines on it.

Tweezers

Not the short, stubby ones with square flat ends that live in the bathroom cabinet. They're good enough to pull out splinters but for building plastic kits we need something altogether different.

Tweezers come in many shapes and sizes, made from plastics, various types and grades of stainless steel, aluminium and other alloys. Medical professionals, jewellers and watchmakers all use tweezers, so you can buy them from scientific instrument suppliers and medical wholesalers as well as modellers' tool suppliers. The specialists listed in Appendix 1 all stock a good range of tweezers.

Which pattern or type should you buy? The most useful are the finely-pointed straight stainless steel type. Choose a pair about five inches long, although a smaller pair will come in handy as well. For the smaller pair, you could probably manage to file points onto an ordinary domestic pair.

The usual arrangement is for tweezers to spring open when pressure on the blades is released; however, the reverse-action type shown in the photograph stay closed until pressure is applied. This type is a very useful addition to the toolbox but is not essential.

Wet'n'dry paper

Wet'n'dry is a colloquialism for the tough, waterproof, carbide abrasive paper used in the automotive finishing industry. The term generally used to indicate its abrasiveness is 'grit'. For our purposes, 120 grit paper is coarse, 240 grit medium and 400 grit fine. 600 grit and above is only used for burnishing out minute scratches and is too fine for use with styrene.

You can buy wet'n'dry paper in most DIY stores, branches of Halfords, auto factors and car accessory shops, and from many decorators' suppliers. Other abrasives come in handy. You can buy flex-ible abrasive strips and sticks called Flex-i-files from some model shops or, failing that, purloin your wife's emery board (the thing she does her nails with). If you haven't got a wife, you can buy emery boards at a chemists.

Vice

Again, another 'nice but not essential' item. Not essential for assembling Ratio kits, that is – you can't do without one for modelling in metal.

I use a small clamp-on bench vice with smooth two-inch jaws. It has its uses when I'm building plastic models, although only for supporting assemblies as they are drying or for preparing metal detail components.

HOME MADE TOOLS

Assembly surface

Often, the model can be erected directly on the work surface but it's much handier to have a squared grid over which to build. In this respect, the green rubber cutting mat would seem to be ideal. But the assembly surface needs to be truly flat and the mat will only be as flat as the bench or table top it is standing on. Besides, it's too flexible to guarantee a level playing field.

The best compromise I have found is to carefully draw a grid (at about quarter-inch increments) in black ink on stout cartridge paper and tape this to a sheet of plate glass. Most glaziers can supply an offcut cheaply. Protect the sharp edges

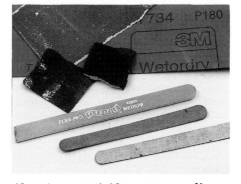

Abrasives: wet'n'dry paper, ordinary manicurists' emery boards and their modelling equivalent, the Flex-i-file.

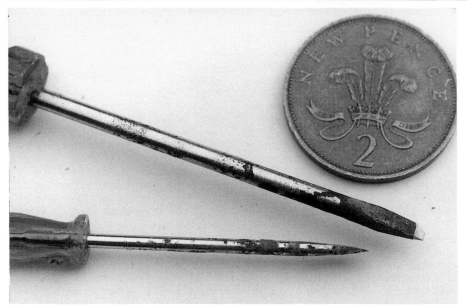

Filed and sharpened small screwdrivers (the smaller the better) can be used on plastic for chiselling, paring, scraping, distressing, texturing and severing. Cheap, easy to make and an absolutely essential tool.

with masking tape. Turn it over and there's your assembly surface.

Another advantage of assembling a model on glass is that the plastic components will tend not to stick to it if you're a little over-generous with the liquid adhesive.

Chisel or parer

This is a really useful, yet simple, tool that you can make for yourself. I consider it an essential, even if you're only intending to assemble the kit straight from the box without modifications.

The photograph tells the whole story, really. To make a paring chisel, you need one of the little electrical screwdrivers which can be bought for a few pence almost anywhere (try Woolworths), a small file and an oilstone. If you haven't got a stone, a sheet of 320 (or finer) grit wet'n'dry on a hard, flat surface will do at a pinch.

Simply file the tip of the screwdriver to a sharp edge and hone it up on the stone. As well as the chisel-shaped tip, you can easily make other versions with 'V' or half-round shaped ends that can be used as gouges. Because the screwdrivers are so cheap, it's easy to experiment and build up a little collection of different types.

I use the chisel (and several similar home-made tools) all the time. You can nip components out of their sprues with a little downward pressure, accurately nibble away edges, pare off moulded surface detail (such as grab handles on carriage sides), scrape material away from tricky corners, square up or open inside angles, scratch or carve relief, add texture to or 'distress' smooth surfaces and a hundred and one similar tasks.

Many experienced modellers use similar tools. You can buy a plastic scriber or 'scrawker', or an artists' scraperboard knife (the sort with a 'V' tip) and I've also seen leather-toolers' knives recommended.

Sanding block

Another essential home made item for

plastic kit building. It is simplicity itself, being no more than a sheet (or sheets) of abrasive paper stuck to a flat board. The 'flat' is the important bit, as the block will be used to true up edges and to level surfaces.

I always use wet'n'dry paper for sanding blocks. The paper itself usually comes as an A4 sheet (A4 is the size of this page) but I find that's a bit big for a sanding block – it takes up too much bench space and is a little unwieldy. Half an A4 sheet (designated, with Eurocratic logic, A5) is a better size for the block – that's about 8ins x 6ins in English.

The block itself can be cut from any flat, firm board such as medium density fibreboard, blockboard, chipboard or plywood. I use 12mm thick Contiboard, which is adequately rigid. The wet'n'dry is simply stuck onto the board with a good contact adhesive, such as Evostick or Thixofix. Some aerosol adhesives will do as well. Make sure the paper is flat on the board with no wrinkles and leave it overnight to allow the glue to set before you use it.

If you are only sticking paper to one side, go for 180 grit. If you've chosen a formica or melamine faced board, glue rubber or sponge pads on the base to prevent it sliding about. Better yet, make the sanding block double sided – 180 grit on one side, 240 or 320 grit on t'other. There's posh.

Finally, don't sharpen pencils on the sanding block. The graphite dust may get transferred onto plastic components where it will not only make a smudgy mess, but stop the paint adhering later. Take it from one who's made the mistake.

The minimum tool kit

How should a newcomer, perhaps building up a tool kit from scratch, reduce the list above to more manageable proportions? Well, an electric minidrill is quite obviously an unnecessary luxury and you can build any plastic kit without owning a Xuron shear. The side cutter is not es-

sential and nor are the spring-close tweezers. The cutting mat is another luxury item.

In the 'scrape by without' category, add the razor saw, the gripping tools except the four-inch pointed tweezers and the files except for the flat and triangular Swiss files. Out goes the little bench vice as well.

You'll almost certainly need the Stanley knife. Although it's possible to cut everything with a small craft knife, the larger tool makes it both easier and safer.

So we come to what I consider the irreducible minimum tool kit needed to assemble a plastic kit with no metal parts.

A small paintbrush to apply solvent adhesive.

A pair of tweezers to hold small parts.

A sharp craft knife or a scalpel.

A home-made chisel or gouge.

A small steel rule.

A square of some sort, preferably a 4ins engineers' square.

A sanding block.

Two sheets of wet'n'dry paper, one 180 grit, the other 320 or 400.

A cutting surface, such as a sheet of thick card with grid lines drawn on.

Although not part of the tool kit, the last essential is a selection of odds and ends such as paper clips, clothes pegs, rubber bands, cocktail sticks, small offcuts of wood and a couple of weights of some sort. All these will make the job easier and safer.

Maintaining tools and saftey

Tools need to be maintained in safe condition. If a file, chisel, saw or knife has a wooden or plastic handle, check regularly that it is clean, in good condition and holds the tool firmly.

A sharp tool will cut the work but a blunt one will only cut you. Blunt cutting tools are more likely to slip or skid than sharp ones and blunt saws are prone to jam. Slipping, skidding and jamming tools will usually slip, skid or jam into *you*.

It only takes a moment to change the blade of a scalpel, craft knife or Stanley knife. Razor saws (and other small modellers' saws) aren't worth sharpening. Once they are blunt, simply replace them.

Files blunt eventually and although they *can* be sharpened it is far more practical to replace them. But don't let them get clogged up with detritus. That will stop them cutting and make them skid. Light rust can be brushed off with a brass-bristled suede brush but if files (or any other tools) become heavily corroded, it is safer to throw them away.

It is reasonably safe to use small Swiss files without a handle fitted because the 'handle' end is usually rounded. Even so, it is worth buying a clip-on handle to hold small files.

When it comes to larger files, it's a different story. These have a protruding, tapered spike (called a tang) which is there to secure a handle. *Never* use a tang-ed file without a proper handle. If you do, you'll probably end up with the tang buried in the palm of your hand.

Some of the cutting tools modellers use are extremely sharp. It takes *very* little pressure to sink a pointed 10A scalpel blade half-an-inch into flesh. That's deep enough to reach many arteries of the forearm, wrist and hand. Therefore, always work in such a way that if the tool should slip or skid, it will miss you and the soft, messy stuff you're made of.

The cardinal rule is to *always* cut away from your free hand. Expressed another way, always keep your free hand *behind* the cutting edge. This may mean turning the workpiece on the bench, inverting it or using clamps (rather than your hand) to hold it.

Wherever possible, cut away from your body as well. By skewing your chair or turning the workpiece you can usually arrange things so that if the knife slips it will pass to one side of your chest rather than into it.

You will often need to cut or score a straight line. The safe way is to run the knife, away from you, along a steel rule. Make sure you hold the rule *behind* the cutting edge.

When cutting with knives of any kind, never exert too much pressure. The blade will be far more likely to either jam or slip if you do. If you bear down too hard on a scalpel or small craft knife, the thin blade may snap and fly off. If it hurtles into your eye, you're in real trouble.

When you're sawing, keep your free hand from under the blade. If the workpiece breaks, the saw slips or the cut suddenly breaks through, you'll have a nicely serrated gash.

The same cautions apply to drill bits. They are cutting tools, too. If you press too hard, they'll break and if they slip off the work you'll be surprised at how easily the smaller sizes penetrate your flesh. Up to the chuck with no bother at all.

Even if the workpiece is in the vice when you are cutting, sawing, filing or drilling, keep your free hand clear and don't sit so that your thigh is directly below the work.

Sometimes, you may be modelling with the work on a board or tray on your lap. In the workshop, your hands, face and chest are most at risk; with a tray, your thighs and abdomen also come into the firing line. If possible, do the easier bits on your lap but take the heavier cutting jobs to the bench or table.

If you're using a low voltage mini drill with a slitting disc or circular saw blade to cut components, make sure the workpiece is firmly supported and secured by a clamp or vice. Keep your hands well clear of the rotating tool. Wear goggles or safety spectacles when using carborundum slitting discs. Occasionally the discs shatter and send sharp bits flying into your face.

Electrical safety

The UK domestic supply is usually around 230-240 volts and each outlet on the ring main is designed to provide up to 13 amps. Thirteen amps at 240V is potentially lethal. *Mains electricity can – and often does – kill!*

There are three lines of defence for you and your tools; adequate earthing, appropriate fuses, and a leakage protection device.

Always ensure that the power supply to your home is properly earthed. Your local electricity company will often check this free of charge. Some hand power tools, lamps and similar appliances have an earth wire in their leads. Others don't because they are double insulated. If there *is* an earth wire, make sure it is connected to the earth pin in the plug.

Next is the fuse in the plug. Unfortunately, many plugs are sold fitted with a fuse rated at 13A. This is too high – a mains electric drill needs a 5A fuse *at most* and a lamp should be fitted with a fuse rated at 3A or less. Wattage is volts times amps so a small soldering iron will run with a fuse rated at less than a quarter of an amp. Fit a 1A mains cartridge fuse to the iron's plug; you can buy them from some specialist electrical retailers and computer stores. The fuse and earth are not enough by themselves. The most essential safety feature is a protection device called a 'current operated earth leakage circuit breaker'. Many modern consumer units (that's the distribution board with the meter and fuses) are fitted with one. It's sometimes referred to simply as a 'leakage trip' or a circuit breaker. If your home has one, it will have a test button. Test it periodically. If it doesn't work, call your electricity supplier.

Current operated earth leakage circuit breakers that plug into a standard mains socket are also available. They are sold in DIY shops, Woolworths, many supermarkets and most electrical goods retailers. They cost about a tenner. That's a lot cheaper than a reasonably modest funeral at about £1,500. You plug this sort of earth leakage circuit breaker into the wall socket then plug your tool or extension lead into it.

If you don't have built-in earth leakage protection on your consumer unit, *always* use one of the plug-in type for your tools and lamps or the extension lead which supplies them. Even if you have a built-in one, the plug-in type are more sensitive and offer greater protection, so use both for belt-and-braces. I always do.

Any tool, or lamp, must have the switch on the positive side of the supply. If you fit an auxiliary switch (to an extension lead, a wander lamp or the mains lead of a soldering iron, for example) it *must* be on the live side. That is, on the brown or red wire.

Keep your extension leads in good condition. Make sure the cord grip (where the lead enters a trailing socket or plug) is tightened. If the insulation is damaged, replace the lead – never bodge it up with insulation tape. In use, make sure that the lead is kept away from heaters, doesn't get pinched by doors and isn't placed where it will trip you up.

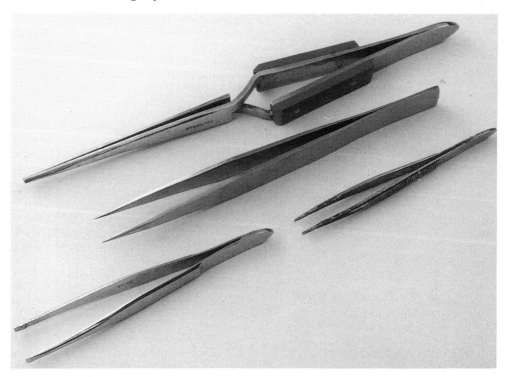

The more the merrier when it comes to tweezers. The top pair is self closing. In the centre is the most useful type, finely pointed, five-inch, stainless steel. At a push, you can scrounge the bottom two from your wife's cosmetic bag.

Chapter Four
MATERIALS

You need very few materials to assemble a Ratio model if you build it 'straight from the box' (that is, without any additions or modifications). But once you start to add detail, adapt or modify your kit, you'll need things that don't come in the packet.

These include styrene in sheet, strip and rod forms, wire, and all the other odds and ends modellers usually describe as 'scrapbox' materials. But whether you want to enhance a kit or stick to the straight and narrow, you'll need adhesives. So I'll start with them.

ADHESIVES

The principal operation in assembling a Ratio kit is uniting the components. The joints are made using an appropriate adhesive. As this book is aimed at the comparative newcomer, I will describe the various types in some depth. The techniques of using them are described in Chapter 5.

There are several different sorts of bond you may need to make; plastic to plastic, metal to plastic and fibrous or absorbent materials to plastic. Each needs a different sort of adhesive and within each group there are plenty of brands to choose from.

Choosing the wrong glue (or using the right one badly) is the most common pitfall for the newcomer, so it is important to use the best adhesive for the particular job in hand and to use it correctly. Among the more frequent mistakes are: applying too much liquid adhesive or using the fiercest when a gentler one would do the job better; swamping small delicate components; trying to stick metal components to plastic with polystyrene cement; and using copious amounts of superglue straight from the tube.

Liquid solvent adhesives

When I was a lad, we all used polystyrene cement (the clear stringy stuff in a tube) to build our Airfix Spitfires. But times change. Nowadays, liquid adhesives are the most popular and convenient way of assembling plastic kits.

Liquid adhesives for styrene are chemicals of a class called organic solvents. They are supplied in glass bottles. The capacity varies between brands, from about 25ml to 50ml. You can buy some brands in larger sizes but a 50ml bottle is sufficient to assemble dozens of kits if used sparingly. Like any chemicals, they are safe if used sensibly but you should read, and follow, the safety advice below.

Some brands of liquid adhesive come with a brush attached inside the screw cap of the bottle. Beware of these built-in brushes. Their stubby, stiff bristles will almost certainly carry too much adhesive to the job and you'll have scant control over where it goes. Cut the brush off the cap and use a small paint brush to apply the adhesive as described elsewhere.

Ratio recommends and supplies Polsol Liquid Polystyrene Adhesive. However, you'll have to visit the factory or look out for the exhibition stand if you want to buy it direct from them; Ratio won't send chemicals through the post. Your local model shop should be able to order it for you, however.

Polsol comes in a 50ml bottle, the screw cap of which *doesn't* incorporate a brush for applying (an omission that I consider a plus point). At the time of writing (January 1996) the price is £1.45, making it one of the cheapest brands. The label carries full hazard warnings and clearly identifies the contents as butanone (also known as methyl ethyl ketone), one of the less volatile solvents.

Daywat Poly is another popular brand based on butanone. Like Polsol, it is reasonably effective on hard plastics, although it is best on styrene. It is available from many model shops.

MekPak, marketed by Slaters, took its name from **m**ethyl **e**thyl **k**etone, the original constituent. Today, MekPak is trichloroethane. It is a good general purpose styrene adhesive and is sold by many model shops.

Humbrol Liquid Poly adhesive is probably the most widely available liquid adhesive and is on sale in most model, toy and craft shops. Formerly based on trichloroethane, it now contains a milder solvent called butyl acetate. This means it is not as active as most other brands and therefore less likely to mar the surface of clear styrene glazing sheet.

Plastic Weld, on the other hand, is pretty fierce in its action. It is one of the few liquid adhesives that is really effective on hard ABS plastics. It has a very volatile solvent, dichloromethane, as its active ingredient so take particular care to ensure adequate ventilation when using it. It is usually sold alongside the Plastruct range of ABS sections.

There are quite a few other brands on the market but those listed above are the ones generally used by railway modellers. So which should you choose?

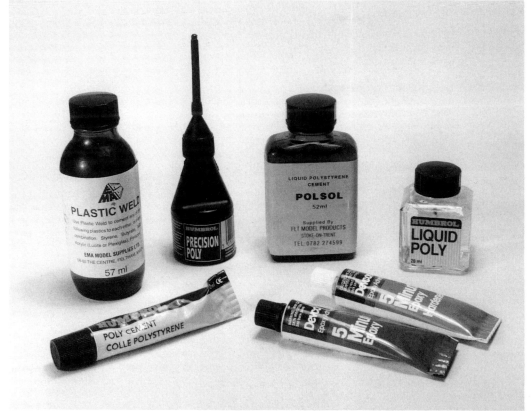

You'll need different adhesives for different jobs.

I like to have three different liquid adhesives to hand when I'm building a kit. For general construction I rely on one containing butanone, usually Polsol. For jobs where something gentler is called for, especially for working with transparent glazing material, I use Humbrol Liquid Poly. Finally, I keep a bottle of Plastic Weld on the bench. It's a bit fierce for most styrene construction, but invaluable for the harder ABS type of plastics or for jobs where you need real bite.

Whichever type or brand of liquid adhesive you buy, read the label and take heed of any safety advice. Don't buy a brand which doesn't clearly identify the contents and carry COSHH (Care Of Substances Hazardous to Health) safety information and hazard warnings on the label.

If you come across a solvent (or other modelling chemical) on sale that does not identify the contents or carry COSHH labelling, you should complain to your local Trading Standards Officer – you'll find his number in Yellow Pages.

Solvent safety

Any organic solvent is potentially dangerous. Most are toxic and they should all be handled sensibly. Although the safety precautions below apply to adhesives, most of the advice also applies to solvents used for thinning paints.

Many of the harmful side effects of chemicals are not discovered until the substances have been in use for some time, so what seems innocuous today could turn out to be tomorrow's cancer agents. Therefore, treat all solvents as hazardous and always err on the side of caution.

The main danger is inhalation of the vapour because most of these chemicals are volatile and evaporate quickly. Breathing the fumes, even in small concentrations, can induce headache or drowsiness. Breathing greater concentrations may produce the same symptoms more rapidly, and in extreme cases lead to hallucination, unconsciousness and even death.

Always store your solvent adhesive out of the reach of youngsters. Do not leave children alone with open bottles of *any* chemical. Some brands of solvent adhesive are sold in bottles with childproof caps. If yours isn't and you have small children around, decant the solvent into a glass childproof bottle. You can buy these at larger chemists shops.

Solvents that are effective on plastic will also be effective on your skin. By dissolving natural oils and fats, they may cause painful drying and cracking. Liquid adhesives can also exacerbate, or cause, rashes and eczema, so always try to avoid skin contact with them.

The three basic safety rules are:

Always ensure adequate ventilation. Don't inhale the vapour of evaporating solvent, or solvent spray mist. Keep the cap on the bottle when not actually using the solvent. Take care to ensure the bottle or jar will not easily be tipped over.

Do not smoke while using solvents. Always keep any organic solvent away from naked flames, soldering irons or other sources of heat. Store solvents in tightly sealed, labelled containers in a safe place away from heat or direct sunlight.

Never mix different solvents together. However, the less active types (including Polsol) can be used to 'dilute' polystyrene cement as described in Chapter 5.

Polystyrene cement

I said earlier that liquid adhesive had eclipsed the old-fashion tube of glue. Well, it is only a partial eclipse. The old stager still has its uses and these are described in Chapter 5.

There are several brands to choose from, the most popular being Humbrol Poly Cement. You can buy this in almost any toy, hobby or model shop.

Humbrol Precision Poly

This product falls neatly between the liquid adhesives and the 'traditional' tube of polystyrene cement.

Precision Poly is a gel, thicker than liquid adhesive but thinner than tube cement. It comes in a squeezable black plastic container with a length of bright steel capillary tubing, protected by a plastic sleeve, extending from the top. With a little practice and care, you can feed the adhesive into a joint or deposit a tiny drop in otherwise inaccessible places.

The label doesn't carry any hazard symbols or safety warnings but Humbrol are generally very careful about such things so it is unlikely to be a COSHH-listed chemical. It's certainly not very fierce in its action.

Cyanoacrylates ('superglues')

Any of the adhesives listed above will successfully bond styrene but several of Ratio's kits also include metal components. Examples include the chain on the water crane, the walkway on the oil storage depot and some of the signal kit components. You may also wish to use metal to add your own details, including sheet brass or nickel silver, steel or brass wire, dress makers' pins and so on.

Ratio's instructions recommend Loctite Superglue Extra for attaching the metal components in the kits. I don't like cyanoacrylate adhesive. I find the quick drying is more often a hindrance than a help but plenty of other modellers get on famously with it.

Superglues come in two forms, liquid and gel, both characterised by very swift bonding action. This is the major drawback of cyanoacrylate; get something in the wrong place and it will probably have to stay there because there's no time for adjustment as the glue sets. And because these adhesives form a very strong joint, you are unlikely to get the offending item off in one piece for another try.

The bond relies on the exclusion of air so the mating surfaces need to be a close fit. The gels are rather more forgiving in this respect and will even bridge very small gaps but the liquid types demand a very close fit of the parts. For the same reason, superglues are not very effective on anything porous or absorbent. Except,

notoriously, human skin. Consider yourself warned. Don't be tempted to squeeze the glue straight onto the work from the nozzle of the plastic bottle. Always decant a drop or two onto a scrap of metal or a tin lid and then use a bit of wire or a cocktail stick to transfer it to the joint.

As a breed, superglues are fussy beasts so read the manufacturers' instructions carefully and abide by them. Superglue is also very expensive (although a little goes a long way) so it's worth storing and using it properly.

Epoxy resin adhesives

Quick-setting epoxy resin adhesive (the best known brand is Araldite) is probably the best choice for sticking metal to plastic. On the plus side, epoxy bridges gaps, fills crevices, sticks like the proverbial to a blanket, allows plenty of time for minor adjustment and is easy to work with. Against that, it is not particularly cheap, especially as one always seems to mix up more than the job needs which means a fair bit of wastage, and some brands are stringy and can be messy. Epoxy also smells unpleasant and doesn't take paint too well.

Epoxy adhesives consist of two components that must be mixed together. They usually come in tubes, one containing the actual resin and the other an agent, called the hardener, which chemically cures the adhesive. So the two components must be kept apart until needed. Equally obviously, the cap from one tube must not be put on the other but they are usually coded in some way.

The original Araldite took 24 hours to set firmly at normal room temperature; quick-setting epoxy takes less than a quarter of an hour. However, neither type will reach its final strength in those times. Even the 'five minute' type takes an hour or more to fully cure.

The chemical reaction is sensitive to heat – the warmer it gets, the quicker it sets. If you're mending crockery, you can accelerate the curing process dramatically by placing the job in the oven but this is obviously not a good idea with a plastic kit. But it may be worth moving the model near a radiator if your workplace is cold.

However, warmth has another effect. Like oil, the resin becomes thinner as it gets warmer. In fact, some brands that are normally as thick as porridge (and therefore readily stay where you put them) become alarmingly runny if you warm them up. If you've already mixed in the hardener, the warm adhesive may go through a brief liquid stage that lasts just long enough for it to sneak off where it's not wanted then rapidly set solid before you can do anything about it.

There are several brands to choose from. Five Minute Araldite seems thicker than most of the others but, in my experience, it's also a lot more likely to become stringy. My personal favourite is an American brand called Devcon. It has a good consistency, rarely strings and seems generally vice-free. It is not as readily available as Araldite but you can get it from larger model shops, some hardware

Moulded styrene architectural surfaces are indispensable for scratchbuilding, kitbashing and crosskitting. For instance, the excellent vacuum formed arc corrugated iron roof which is included in Ratio kits [231, 232, 525 and 527] can be obtained as a spare moulding in 4mm scale or as item [317] in the 2mm scale Builders Packs range. It can be adapted to many other uses and would be ideal for modelling this dilapidated barn.

stores and, of course, it's usually on sale at the bigger model railway shows.

Other adhesives

Sometimes you will need to bond other materials to styrene. When it comes to adding extra detail, you may want to use balsa or other woods, card, paper, scenic scatter, foliage mat and so on. These materials call for something other than liquid adhesive, superglue or epoxy.

Contact adhesives such as UHU, Bostik Clear, Evostick and Thixofix are useful for sticking paper or card to plastic and for attaching scenic materials. The first two can be obtained from either stationery or hardware shops, the others from DIY stores or builders' merchants.

More specialised adhesives can also be used to attach scenic materials. Cow Gum is a rubbery, tacky adhesive used in graphics studios for paste-up work. Apply it sparingly to the area of the model you want 'vegetated' and press the greenery down into it. Unfortunately, it dries with a noticeable rubbery sheen. Another useful product is aerosol contact adhesive, also used in studios. The best known brands are Spray Mount and Photo Mount. With aerosols, it's the foliage rather than the building that gets the glue. Hold it in the tweezers, blast it with the aerosol then dab it into place.

Use any contact adhesive sparingly (especially Evostick) because the solvent can attack styrene. Keep the lid on the tin (or the cap on the tube) as all these adhesives dry out easily, and none of them are cheap.

Occasionally, metal parts can be attached with contact adhesives if the joint has a relatively large surface area and bears no load. The bond will not be very strong and it is better to use either two part epoxy or cyanoacrylate to attach metal fittings.

That just about covers adhesives. Let's recap. For joining styrene, use Polsol or MekPak; for glazing, use Humbrol

Liquid Poly; for harder plastics, use Plastic Weld; and for certain jobs use polystyrene cement or Humbrol Precision Poly. For contact adhesion, use Evostick, UHU or a spray adhesive. For metals use either Loctite Superglue Extra or Devcon two part epoxy adhesive.

If you are a newcomer, you need to gather the basics together without spending too much at one go. I recommend a 50ml bottle of Polsol or MekPak, a small tube of UHU and a pack of Devcon. If you can't get hold of the Devcon, Araldite Rapid is an acceptable substitute.

OTHER MATERIALS

Ratio kits contain all the components needed to build a 'standard' model. But you will have to find additional materials for any modifications or substitutions that suggest themselves to you.

The footbridge kits, for instance, do not have moulded handrails. If you want to remedy this omission, you'll have to get some brass wire or plastic rod from another source. Similarly, although the water crane comes with a nice looking length of rigid etched brass 'chain', substituting a length of Slaters' flexible miniature chain will maker it look even better.

The material you will need most often is polystyrene, in sheet, strip and rod form. As it is the same raw material as Ratio uses, it's obviously totally compatible with the kits – it can be worked with the same tools, joined with the same adhesive and painted with the same paints. Styrene comes in a huge range of size, shape and colour combinations from several sources.

Other useful materials include wire and rod, foil, metal in various other forms, balsa wood, card, paper, fillers and modelling clay. Some of these need to be bought but many can come from the scrap box.

Armed with all these materials, you can add a great deal of extra detail to your models, giving them a unique character and individuality.

Styrene sheet

This is the basic material. There is a bewildering range of styrene sheet sizes, thicknesses and textures available from a plethora of craft and hobby, commercial and industrial sources. Things will be simpler if you choose from the two ranges most often used by railway modellers, Slaters and Evergreen.

First, the smooth, untextured stuff. Slaters is the most readily available. It is sold under the brand name Plastikard, although 'plasticard' with a small 'p' has now become a generic term for similar products from any manufacturer. You can buy Plastikard in most model railway shops, at exhibitions, direct from Slaters or from many mail order suppliers. Evergreen is a little harder to track down; a good source is John K Flack whose address is in Appendix 1.

You can narrow the choice down even more by sticking to the 'standard' sheet size. For Slaters, this is 330mm x 220mm (a little larger than A4, the size of this book). Evergreen sheets come in similar sizes. Of course, larger sheets are available from both Slaters and Evergreen.

When it comes to sheet thickness, there is plenty of choice. Both Evergreen and Slaters list the thicknesses in thousandths of an inch or 'thou'. Forty thou (which is expressed in figures as 0.040ins or ·040") is equivalent to one millimetre. Both ranges offer 10, 15, 20, 30, 40, 60 and 80thou thicknesses. The most useful to start with are 10, 20 and 40thou but Slaters offer a useful assorted pack containing one sheet each of 10, 15, 20, 30, 40 and 60thou in white for under a fiver.

The standard colour is white but most thicknesses come in black as well, although this is usually restricted to the larger sheet sizes. Slaters also do a range of coloured sheets in 20thou.

Textured styrene sheet

There are two main ranges of architectural surface styrene sheets. Slaters em-

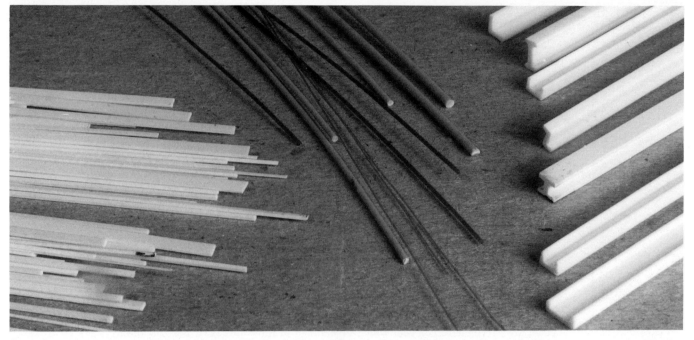

Styrene comes in many shapes and sizes. On the left, an assorted pack of Slaters microstrip provides a generous selection of flat and square sections. In the centre, microrod of various diameters, which can also be bought as an assorted pack. On the right is a very small selection from the huge range of angles, channels and girders in the Fineline Styrene range.

bossed sheets are slightly smaller than the plain Plastikard at 300mm x 174mm. They are produced for 2mm, 4mm and 7mm scales and include common surfaces such as brickwork, stone, planking, granite setts, cobblestones and roof tiles. Many of these sheets are available in a choice of colour.

The other range of textured styrene sheets is the Wills Scenic Series. The sheets are moulded rather than embossed, giving stronger detail than the Slaters equivalent, and are only available in 4mm scale.

The Wills sheets also differ from Slaters in size and thickness. They are much smaller, about 5ins x 3ins, which means an unsightly joint if you need a large area such as a roof. Their thickness, 2mm, is both a blessing and a curse. On the one hand, it makes cutting a chore, especially intricate shapes like doorways or windows. Against this, the material is very rigid and so needs little support.

Wills offers a slightly wider range of surfaces than Slaters, including brickwork, various types of stone walling, tile and slate roofing and so on – over two dozen in all. The surface detail is much heavier than on the Slaters embossed sheets and slightly overscale in many cases. However, this means that the ranges are to some extent complementary. For instance, to represent new or well-maintained flush-pointed brickwork, the Slaters product would be the better choice. But for more decrepit brickwork, perhaps a barn, an old cottage or an enclosing wall, the Wills sheet would be more appropriate.

Both the Slaters and Wills textured ranges are compatible with Ratio kits and by combining the three firms' products, a huge range of possibilities is opened up.

Microrod and Microstrip

Both these products are absolutely invaluable for adding detail to plastic models.

Microrod is small round-section styrene 'wire'. It has a multitude of uses and is manufactured by both Slaters and Evergreen. The Slaters variety (listed as Plastic Rod) is available in diameters from 10thou to 50thou (0.25mm to 1.25mm) and you can buy an assorted pack containing two dozen lengths for under £2.

Microstrip refers to lengths of small rectangular section styrene. Although a Slaters brand name, the word is often used generically to describe similar products from other manufacturers, notably Evergreen.

Microstrip comes in a wide variety of width/thickness combinations, ranging from 10thou x 20thou (approximately 0.25mm x 0.5mm) to 276thou x 60thou (approximately 7mm x 1.5mm). The handiest way to buy it is as an assorted pack. Slaters offer 50 strips of various sizes, again for less than £2.

Slaters, Wills and Evergreen products are available from the suppliers listed in Appendix 1. You may also find it useful to get hold of their catalogues which list all the sizes and textures available.

Fineline Styrene

Fineline Styrene is an American range of plastic sections, similar to the earlier Plastruct, designed for architectural and engineering model making.

Plastruct has the drawback of being made from ABS, a hard plastic resistant to many liquid adhesives and therefore difficult to bond to styrene. Fineline, however, is moulded in white styrene and so is fully compatible with Ratio's mouldings and the Slaters, Evergreen and Wills products.

The range consists of angles (8 sizes); shallow channels (7 sizes); deep channels (5 sizes); 'T' sections (6 sizes); 'H' sections (8 sizes), 'I-beam' sections (12 sizes); 'Z' sections (5 sizes); oblong tubes (3 sizes); square tubes (5 sizes); round tubes (8 sizes), and half-round sections (3), as well

as a range of styrene sheet and strip. There are also special items such as 'light gathering' acrylic rods and polycarbonate sheets, and a small selection of styrene architectural items such as stairs, ladders and railings. These last are ideally suited to industrial and architectural scratchbuilding as well as for detailing and kitbashing Ratio products.

Fineline Styrene is distributed by EMA Model Supplies and is sold from purpose-made display units in many model, craft, art and hobby shops. EMA do not normally supply direct to the public, but if you have difficulty in finding a supplier or want a price list, send a stamped SAE to the address in Appendix 1.

Scrapbox materials

A modeller should never throw anything away. Although this advice isn't intended to be taken literally, it's worth saving all sorts of oddments that might come in handy even if you can't see a use for them at the time. That's how you build up a scrapbox.

When you build plastic kits, there are often alternative parts supplied. Save them. To take a non-railway example for a change, the 1:48 scale Airfix Spitfire kit contains two patterns of windshield, two types of radiator scoop, alternative cannons and the undercarriage can be modelled lowered or retracted. All the spare bits from a kit like that are fodder for your scrapbox. You may not see a use for them immediately but they'll come in handy someday.

Often, the kit's sprues contain usable material, such as short cylindrical sections. Many Ratio kit sprues have a small flat panel with the company's name moulded on it. Cut these off and save them. They make useful bases and can also be used for bracing internal corners.

Other plastic items suggest modelling uses. The plastic shafts of cotton buds,

Gate fixtures, fences, notice board posts, signal wire pulleys, raised conduits - the sort of details that call for microstrip, microrod and styrene sections.

plastic drinking straws and insulation sleeving from all sorts of wire can represent drainpipes, gutters, cable conduit and many other things.

Small items of metal scrap have a multitude of uses. Offcuts of straight brass wire, the copper core of twin-and-earth electrical cable, spare fusewire, unused etched components and fret waste are all useful. Bent drawing pins, dressmakers' pins, the brass bolts, washers and other components from damaged three-pin plugs - all these are treasure trove for modellers. Small glass beads and tiny buttons can be pressed into service, too.

Keep unused transfers from kits (you usually get several choices of running number with wagons or alternative regimental brandings with military vehicles) together with part-used sheets of Meccanorma and Letraset dry transfer lettering.

You'll find it useful to organise this collection. Stash the various types of scrap together – metal oddments in one container, etched fret waste in another, spare plastic bits and pieces in a third. You can

use any suitable container; mine include tobacco tins, 'zip top' polybags, shoe boxes and other small card cartons. The boxes that the larger Ratio kits are supplied in are excellent. Perhaps the most ubiquitous and useful containers are the plastic tubs in which margarine or ice cream is sold. Wash them out and keep them. They come in handy for all sorts of things as well as storing your odds and ends.

Don't put too much scrap in each tub or box. That way, you'll be able to see at a glance what you've got and you won't have to turf everything out on to the bench to extract a particular goodie.

Wire

The oddments of wire in your scrapbox are likely to be short or kinked or, more often than not, both. Longer, straighter lengths are needed for making handrails and similar items.

Brass wire is the most useful. It is reasonably rigid, easy to work and solders very readily. The best source is Alan Gibson (see Appendix 1) who sells straight brass wire in 300mm (about

twelve inches) lengths. There are several diameters to choose from; the most versatile are 0.45mm and 0.7mm.

Fuse wire is another modellers' standby. You can buy a card containing three diameters (for 5A, 10A and 13A fuseways) from Woolworth's or DIY stores.

Fillers

Fillers are used, as the name suggests, to fill gaps. Some brands of plastic kits call for more filling than others. Ratio products are very good in this respect. The design of the kits and the quality of manufacture ensure that the components fit closely and accurately.

There will be probably be little call for filler if you are simply assembling a Ratio kit as intended, although you may not achieve a perfect joint every time. But once you start modifying the components or adding extra details, filling will probably become necessary.

Some fillers are designed especially for modellers. One of the most popular is Milliput but Humbrol also do a body putty and there are several others. You can buy them in many hobby and craft shops, model railway specialist retailers and at model railway exhibitions. Failing these sources, try the mail order specialists listed in Appendix 1.

Automotive fillers are another option. Go for the two-pack cellulose type. The best known is Davids P38 Isopon but there are other brands. You'll find a selection in Halfords or your local auto factors. Another readily available filler is Plastic Padding. Some modellers find these types don't adhere to plastics as well as the purpose-made modelling products.

For making good very small blemishes or for filling very narrow gaps, I've seen the following trick recommended. Collect the styrene shavings and dust that result from filing or rubbing down and mix it with a little liquid adhesive to produce a paste. This can be applied carefully from the inside to fill gaps.

Blu Tak

This isn't strictly a 'material' because it isn't used as part of the finished model. But it's very useful stuff to have around the work bench. You can use a sizeable blob to hold the bottle of liquid adhesive down to prevent spillage. Blu Tak is also invaluable for holding or supporting components during assembly and as an undoable adhesive for dry runs.

LICCHT
⊐O◻

Some of the sections, all available in many sizes, from Fineline Styrene. From top, left to right: angles, 'I' beams, shallow channels, deep channels, 'H' girders, 'T' sections, 'Z' sections, square tubes, cylindrical tubes and oblong tubes.

Above: The Ratio station building [204, 504], is one of the larger kits and is based on the prototype at Castle Cary. Extension canopies [205, 208, 225, 515, 516] and modular station platform mouldings [209, 210, 520] are also available in the range. This view includes Ratio's GWR signal box, GWR square post stop signal and loading gauge [411].

Below: The other side of Ratio's station building, photographed in idyllic rural isolation.

Chapter Five
TECHNIQUES

Assembly order

To a large extent the design of the kit dictates the order of assembly, so usually it is perfectly satisfactory to simply follow Ratio's instructions. But if, having familiarised yourself with the kit as suggested in Chapter 2, you feel a different sequence will be more suitable, by all means follow it. The important things are to have a clear plan for the whole process before you start and to make sure that the sequence will be workable.

With some kits, it will be OK to cut all the components from the sprues at the outset, preparing and refining them in one go. With others, it may be best to remove each component or group of components only when needed.

Sometimes it will prove easier to add details and fittings while the main components are unassembled – installing windows in the wall of a building, for instance. Texturing and distressing, especially of small items, may be easier to do before the component is parted from the sprue. Some groups of components may logically make up into complete sub-assemblies.

Painting, often thought of as an entirely separate operation to be undertaken at the end of the building process, is often best done as you go along. A case in point is window frames. These are almost always easier to paint before you install them in a building and should certainly be painted before they are glazed. You may wish to substitute your own windows or to adapt the moulded Ratio frames so that the windows are modelled open. Additional jobs like these need planning into the sequence.

Preparing components

The moulded components need a little preparation. Obviously, the first job is to remove them from their sprues. Resist the temptation to twist or wriggle them free, a habit that some people carry over from their childhood Airfix aeroplane days. Doing this risks distorting or damaging the moulding. Always cut the components free.

How you actually make the cut depends, to some degree, on how large the component is, the thickness of the feeds and runners, and how many attachment points there are.

For most small items, the scalpel or craft knife is the best bet. You should cut through the feed at the thinnest point. If you are reasonably confident, cut as near to the component as possible thus minimising further tidying up. Otherwise, cut a little further back and pare the resulting protrusion flush afterwards.

I often cut small items from the sprue with the little home made chisel. With the workpiece well supported, simply position the blade over the feed and press down firmly. Practise first though and, until you are confident of success, don't

Some components, such as windows and doors, are easier to paint while they are still attached to the sprue.

chop through too close to the component. Larger components may have substantially thicker, stronger feeds. In a few cases, the runner will extend right into the component with no discernible thin feed at all. For these meatier jobs, you need a meatier tool. You can use your Stanley knife, sidecutters or the Xuron shear. The side cutters will distort the plastic on either side of the cut, so don't get too close to the component and clean up the resulting protrusion later. With the Xuron, you get a good, clean square cut and you can therefore get in much closer.

If you are cutting with the chisel, scalpel, Stanley or craft knife rather than shearing, you'll need to support the workpiece on a solid surface. The blockboard work surface is ideal but the rubber cutting mat will have too much give. Sometimes, a large extraction pip on the sprue will tend to raise the feed you want to sever from the cutting surface. If so, position the moulding so that the offending protrusion overhangs the edge of the board, as shown in the photograph.

Small components with thin feeds will come away fairly easily with a steady pressure on the knife. Heavier sections are best cut through with a rocking action. It is important not to try to slice through a thick feed or runner by bearing down heavily. Too much force may cause the knife to slip, the blade to snap or result in damage to the component.

Larger sprues with thicker runners can be chopped into more manageable pieces using the side cutter.

Once you have removed a component, it will need cleaning up. There will be nibs and tabs to remove where the feeds have been cut and there may also be extraction pips to be dealt with.

There are two ways to get rid of unwanted protrusions. You can either cut or pare them with the scalpel, craft knife or (sometimes) the home made chisel or you can rub them down on the sanding block. For smaller items, or on inside edges, the knife or chisel are the obvious choices but for long, unobstructed edges, the sanding block is best.

Finally, there may be moulding flash around some areas of a component. This is a wafer thin 'halo' of styrene, the result of molten plastic squeezing its way between the two pieces of the mould tool. Because it is so thin, it's usually very easy to pare away with the scalpel but occasionally it forms in awkward corners and is more of a fiddle to remove.

Refining components
The first task is to check all the mating surfaces for a good fit. This need not entail a full dry run – simply offer up the pairs of components. Mitred corner joints – the walls of a building or the sides and ends of a wagon – need particular scrutiny. If the joint is mitred, a pass over the sanding block will usually ensure a snug fit.

There may be mould part-lines visible on the components. These are usually along an edge (or round all the edges) of a component.

Often the part-line will be somewhere that won't show on the completed model, in which case it may be possible to leave it. Sometimes a part line runs along an edge that forms a mating face. The sanding block is probably the best remedy in this case.

With a round component, such as telegraph poles, the part-line may be quite obtrusive. A combination of scraping with the scalpel and rubbing down with a loose piece of wet'n'dry paper is the answer here.

This is also the time to thin down any over-thick edges, reduce the depth of window frames, square up inside corners and so on. Some components will have a slight taper to aid extraction from the mould tool and this may need squaring up. Deep-

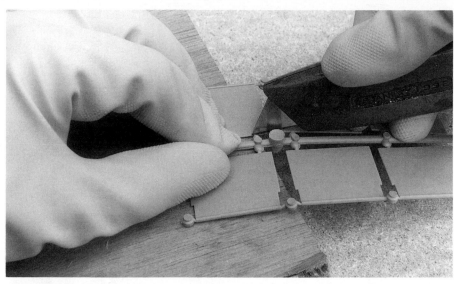

The moulding is held over the edge of the workboard so that the large extraction pip doesn't prevent it laying flat as the feeds are cut.

The Xuron shear can get in really close. In this case, it is being used to nip off extraction pips virtually flush.

ening surface texture, accentuating relief and distressing are part of the refining process. Removing, or substituting, moulded details can be done at this stage, too.

Using liquid adhesive
Put simply, liquid adhesives for plastic work by dissolving the surfaces of the two components to be joined so that they fuse together. The solvent has a fairly low boiling point and evaporates rapidly at room temperature. As it does so, the plastic rehardens, forming a strong rigid bond.

Unlike polystyrene cement, liquid adhesive has no bridging or filling properties. If it is to make a bond, the surfaces to be united must be touching each other. So it is necessary to set the joint up before applying the adhesive (the opposite

Refining detail. The lower moulding of each pair is as it comes, the upper ones have had the cusp removed from the edges and the mortar courses have been deepened and carried round.

Refining joints. Wet'n'dry paper, a touch of filler and the little chisel have been used to round off the corner and continue the mortar courses, disguising the joint on the lower of these two buttresses. The upper buttress awaits treatment so the joint is very noticeable.

to the usual procedure with cement). Once the components are in position, the liquid adhesive should be carried to the joint and applied with a brush. I use a small (size 1 or 0) artists' paint brush as described in Chapter 3. Because it is very 'searching', the liquid runs from the brush into and along the joint by capillary action. In fact, it shoots off like a rat up a drainpipe.

This propensity to flow freely has two drawbacks. Firstly, it is difficult to 'tack' two components together at just one point along their length. Second, any excess liquid will tend to spread out over the surfaces next to the joint. It is therefore *important not to overload the brush*.

If liquid adhesive *does* flood the surface, it will damage it. A thin wash that evaporates away quickly will leave no more than a sheen on the surface but a more substantial amount may destroy detail or texture. It may also produce a very distinct texture of its own, either a stippled effect or a sort of rippling. Even a small amount of adhesive will cause the surface to soften and become tacky; if it is inadvertently handled before it fully rehardens, it will mark badly and may 'string'.

A real flood of solvent may soften the whole component and distort it. Small or thin items are particularly vulnerable; for example, the glazing bars of windows may droop. If no distortion has taken place after a major spillage, all may not be lost. The component will eventually set hard again and the surface can be smoothed down and, if necessary, re-detailed.

If liquid adhesive gets onto the surface of the transparent plastic sheet commonly used to glaze model windows, it may render it translucent. This effect can be exploited if we wish to produce a frosted window such as those in the lavatory compartments of carriages or in the signal box 'privy' (assuming the box *has* a loo standing beside it – many did – and that it is one which boasts a window).

The ill effects of excess or misplaced liquid adhesive will depend to some extent on the type of solvent; some are more active than others and some evaporate more slowly.

To avoid any of these problems, the golden rule is to apply the adhesive sparingly. It is far easier to make a second application if needed than to remedy the effects of too generous a brushload. Don't dip the brush too deeply into the bottle and wipe the excess off on the rim. Once you've loaded the brush, get it to the job quickly or you'll find the adhesive has evaporated (this is less of a problem with Polsol and other butanone adhesives than with fiercer, more volatile ones).

The effects of a brushload going astray are bad enough – image what damage the whole bottle can do. If you've just spent hours preparing the components to perfection and intricately assembling them, you'll not be best pleased to see them dissolve when you accidentally tip 50ml of adhesive over them.

Why court such a disaster? You can easily make a little stand for the bottle from scrap wood or buy one of the commercially produced ones. Failing that, a large dollop of Blu Tak, plasticene or modelling clay to support the bottle is better than nothing. And always screw the cap firmly back onto the bottle unless you're actually loading the brush, even though it may be a fiddle with the brush in one hand and a part-assembled model in the other.

Getting things square

It is important to ensure that the basic structure of a model is truly square. The walls of a building or the sides and end of a wagon or carriage should be vertical and at right angles to each other.

The best way of ensuring that the model sits level and is free of twist is to build it on a sheet of glass, as described in Chapter 3. This has the added advantage that if any liquid adhesive runs down a vertical joint and onto the assembly surface, it will not form a very strong bond with the glass. If you are working on a card surface or a cutting mat, you may well find your kit has gained an inseparable and unplanned base.

When you are assembling a pair of walls at a right angle, the vertical alignment often takes care of itself. Nonetheless, it is as well to use the engineers' square (or an accurately squared block of wood) to ensure that a wall or wagon side is truly perpendicular.

In plan view, squareness sometimes relies on a base, such as the one supplied with Ratio's GWR signal box kit, or a floor in the case of a wagon or carriage. Often, however, you may want a free-standing model or there will be no base or floor. Then it is up to you to make sure the model is square rather than trapezoid.

If your glass assembly table has a drawn grid taped underneath, this will help set things up square. But there is no substitute for the small engineers' square to check that walls are at right angles to each other.

For a straightforward building, first set up two corner walls as a right angled pair. Make sure they are vertical, that the mating edges are a good fit and get them as near to a right angle as possible by lining them up over the grid. Run some liquid adhesive into the joint. Wait until the adhesive has got a good grip then, while the joint is still soft and has a little flexibility, test the angle with the square and tease the walls in or out as appropriate. If they try to spring back, use a few blobs of Blu Tak, masking tape or a few small weights to hold them at the correct angle until the joint is hard.

If you are building a wagon, van or carriage, the floor should take care of the squareness, but it's worth having a dry run and checking that everything is square before you apply the cement.

Remember that the joint will remain soft for a while after you have applied the adhesive and so the assembly must be left to thoroughly harden before you handle it. Otherwise you risk getting it out of true again. How long a joint needs to set depends on how much adhesive you've applied – the more solvent, the longer the hardening time. This is another reason for applying liquid adhesive sparingly.

OTHER TECHNIQUES

Long cuts by scoring and snapping

If you are building a bog standard Ratio model using the components as they come in the packet, you probably won't need to do any major cutting. But as soon as you start to modify or kitbash the Ratio product or fabricate additional components from styrene sheet, you will need to make longer cuts.

For example, if you intend to extend the little brick hut or weighbridge office by uniting two kits, you may need to cut the walls into sections. Again, the Ratio station platform is fairly wide. To use it for a small country station, you will need to narrow it with a lengthways cut.

Although you can cut right through the thinnest sizes of styrene sheet in one go with a knife drawn along a straight edge, for thicker plain sheet and for moulded components the best technique is scoring and snapping. This is just what its name suggests; you cut, or score, part way through with the knife or scalpel, using a steel rule to ensure a straight line, then flex the material until it snaps along the cut. The sheet should part cleanly along

A mitre box made of strip wood keeps the razor saw at a right angle to the workpiece.

the scored line but the edge may need dressing on the sanding block afterwards, especially if it forms the base of the model or will be butted up to another component.

If the material is very thick, it may be necessary to cut or score on both sides, making sure the cuts are accurately aligned. This works fine for plain sheet because it is easy to make an accurate cut or score across a smooth surface. But it is a lot more difficult where there is a heavy texture or moulded relief on one face of the material. In such circumstances, it is better to use a razor saw.

Long cuts by razor sawing

A razor saw is simply a very small version of the carpenter's tenon saw. Its straight, rigid blade makes it the ideal tool for long straight cuts across moulded sheet components. Provided that the blade is maintained at a right angle to the work, a truly square edge can be achieved, ideal if the component is to be butt jointed along the sawn edge.

The razor saw isn't very effective if used 'freehand', so some sort of guide for the blade will be necessary to keep the cut dead straight. You will also need to hold the work steady or you'll never get an accurate, controlled cut. Here are two suggestions.

The first is borrowed from woodwork, where tenon saws are often used to cut square ends or accurate mitres across strip wood. The strip is held in a mitre box to keep the saw blade vertical and direct it at either 45°, 60° or 90° to the long axis of the workpiece. You can easily adapt this technique and construct a cutting guide from stripwood, as shown in the photograph.

An alternative method that I often use calls for a miniature G clamp. Use the clamp to fix a steel rule or other metal straight edge across the workpiece. This will act as a guide for the saw and also clamp the whole job rigidly to the bench. The photograph should make the method clear.

Remember that a razor saw cut is about 0.5mm wide, so be sure to cut on the waste side.

Paring and scraping

Paring is cutting away unwanted material a little bit at a time. You can use a scalpel or craft knife fitted with a curved blade for paring the thicker feeds from an edge or the little chisel for paring moulded surface detail from a component. Make sure the work is well supported, take very little material off with each pass of the blade and always cut away from your hand.

Scraping is one of the most important techniques in plastic modelling. Basically, it entails drawing the blade of a scalpel or knife edge-on along a surface or edge to remove a fine, even sliver of material.

Scraping is often the quickest and surest way of cleaning up an edge, thinning down a component, sharpening a corner or squaring up an extraction taper. It is also usually the most effective way to re-

An alternative method of using the razor saw. The workpiece and steel rule are clamped to the edge of the bench as described in the text. Notice that the square is to hand.

Scraping is one of the most useful techniques when preparing components. It is one of the few operations where it is sometimes necessary to draw the knife towards your hand.

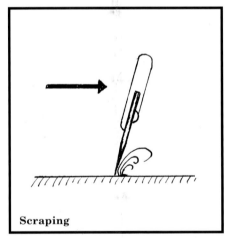

Scraping

move a part-line from a visible surface, especially a round or curved one.

The secret is to hold the knife or scalpel in such a way that the blade is at right angles to the direction in which it is being drawn and angled so as to present a slightly trailing edge to the work. This is easier to demonstrate than to explain but I hope the little sketch and the photograph will make it clear.

Scraping is one of the few operations where it is sometimes necessary to hold the workpiece and draw the knife *towards* your hand (or, more usually, your thumb as shown in the picture). *Be careful.*

It's worth practising scraping on a length of sprue or an offcut of styrene before you set about an actual component. But once you've got the knack, you'll wonder how you managed before.

A short length of sprue has been left projecting from the seat of this tiny chair. The sprue has been bonded to a styrene strip pinned to a block. Thus the seat is firmly supported, leaving both hands free to attach the back and the legs.

Ratio in Colour

Two of the larger Ratio 4mm scale models. Kit [525] is very versatile and in this view (top) it's in the guise of a builders' merchant. The vacuum formed arc roof, available separately in 2mm and 4mm scales, suggests many uses – pig sheds, Nissen huts, Anderson shelters, barns and industrial premises of all kinds. The lower photgraph shows the goods shed kit [534], based on the prototype at Buckfastleigh's preserved station.

Above, my little diorama was inspired by the prototype photographs reproduced on page 41. Drabness is the order of the day here, and the techniques used are described in Chapter Six. Virtually everything in this picture is from Ratio, except for the tools which are Coopercraft mouldings.

Top right, Steve Taylor's variation on the theme – a more rustic setting demands more russet colouring. The graffito is a nice touch.

Centre right, proof that not all grounded carriages need be in an advanced state of decrepitude. This much jollier cameo is the work of veteran modeller Ken Northwood. Ken's layout, the classic 'North Devonshire Railway', has found a temporary home at Ratio's factory. Photo: Leon C Kidd

Right, the concrete hut at Honiton referred to on page 35. Left, my model built from the photograph.

Above, the extended Ratio footbridge on Pecorama's busy Loft Layout. Photo: courtesy of Peco Studios
Left, Ratio's SR concrete subjects (such as the footbridge and the panel fencing) are ideal for modelling recent history and the contemporary scene. Photo: Tony Wright
Below, members of Wolverhampton Model Railway Club obviously like plastic wagon kits – they built these vans and those on the back cover. Photo: Tony Wright

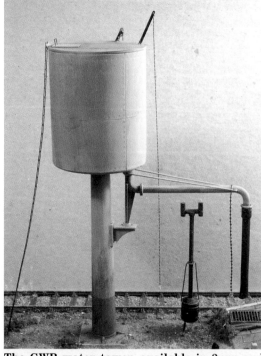

The GWR water tower, available in 2mm and 4mm scales [230, 528].

Ratio's kit [513] for the SR concrete traders' store.

Assembly on the sprue

Occasionally, it is more convenient and practical to make up assemblies before separating a component (or components) from the sprue(s). This is particularly so in the case of very small items.

The example illustrated in the photograph is a 4mm scale chair from a grounded carriage body kit (you get four, if I remember correctly). There are six individual components; the back, legs and rails assemble onto the seat. The problem, of course, is positioning these tiny bits as the liquid adhesive is applied and supporting them while it dries. It is far easier to hold the seat if it is left on its sprue, or, as in the illustration, on part of it.

Dry run

This is simply what it says, a temporary assembly of components to check their location or fit without bonding them.

A dry run will help you familiarise yourself with the assembly sequence. Although Ratio kits include a good exploded diagram and, in most cases, written instructions as well, a dry run can often clarify things that are not immediately obvious from the instruction sheet.

It is always worth testing all mating surfaces against one another before the adhesive comes anywhere near the model. Mostly, Ratio kit components fit together very accurately but a few don't, especially if a feed or runner has to be cut, pared or scraped from the mating faces. If a snug fit relies on three or more components, assembling them dry will be necessary to check that all is well.

If there are only two components to test, you can simply hold them together but when there are several you will need some temporary fixing method. Rubber bands (in as many sizes as you can collect), wire paper clips, 'Dinky' aluminium hair grips,

Distressing to give an impression of decrepitude. The tip of the scalpel and the little chisel are being used to accentuate grain and simulate rot on this door.

Bulldog clips, clothes pegs, Blu Tak and some small weights are all useful here.

Texture

Distressing, adding texture and accentuating relief are often necessary to overcome the limitations of the moulding process and to add character and individuality to the finished model.

You can usually improve the moulded relief. The joints between planks may be deepened with the scriber, for example, or the mortar courses of stonework may look better if you scrape them out to reduce their uniformity. Relief can be reduced as well as emphasised – a window cill may be reduced in thickness or door fittings may be pared away.

Moulded texture may be absent or too light. Take, for instance, the moulded surface of the telegraph poles. They're as smooth as a baby's bottom. A sliver of coarse abrasive paper (say 120 grit) can be wrapped round each pole then drawn down it in a straight line to suggest the grain. This technique is also applicable to other 'unpainted wood' surfaces. Scratching with a scriber, the tip of a scalpel blade or other sharp implement will produce a deeper grain. Gouging with the little chisel can represent patches of rot. Note, however, that wood grain is usually invisible (at least, it is in 4mm scale) on painted woodwork such as doors and window frames.

Distressing is a term borrowed from the antiques business, where it describes the process of artificially introducing the characteristics of age and wear, either to meld restored work into an original set-

A distressed section of the side of a grounded carriage body. The wood grain has been scored in with the tip of the scalpel, the little chisel has been used to pare off the door and grab handles and also to gouge out simulated rot, a section of panelling has been cut out and styrene sheet patches added. It won't look as exaggerated as this once it's had a coat or two of paint.

ting or, less honourably, to produce fakes. In the modelling field, distressing means making something look old, worn or heavily weathered.

The main targets for distressing are those areas of a model which represent timber on the prototype – doors and frames, fence posts, and the like. Grounded carriage and van bodies, as the prototype photographs reproduced in this book show, are suitable candidates for this treatment. Use the tip of the scalpel, the little chisels, a point (the scriber or the tip of a divider or compass) and so on. You can gouge and score deep grain into the wood, cut away planks or boards, produce rot holes or nibble away the bottom of a door or post.

Other surfaces can also be distressed. Brickwork is a good example. Chiselling out, cutting away or roughening individual bricks in a wall can represent flaking and frost damage, the process known as spalling. Corrugated iron sheet (and thin sheet metal generally) often rusts right through, especially around the fastenings and along the lower edges. On roofs, the odd tile or slate can be carefully pared away.

Glazing can also be distressed. Real glass may not rot, but it can crack and break. You can see examples of broken panes, real and model, in the photographs. As with timber, the work can be done with the little chisels, gouges, the point of a scriber or divider and, of course, the scalpel.

Experiment with distressing before you attack a pristine kit component. You can practise on offcuts of styrene sheet or spare mouldings. Always try to work from a prototype photograph.

One final word on distressing. It is very easy to overdo and overuse the technique. Be restrained.

Reinforcing joints

There are two locations where a joint may need reinforcement. The first is inside corner joints, especially walls that need to be kept at right angles to one another. The Ratio station building kits [204, 504] come supplied with little flat corner braces already moulded and these are easy to fabricate for other kits. An alternative is to fit a length of Fineline Styrene angle section, the bigger the better, vertically up the joint.

The other situation where reinforcement is necessary is when you butt joint two components; that is, join two flat pieces end to end. For example, if you are joining two brick hut kits [535] together to make a longer single building you will have to lengthen two walls in this way. On plain walls, you simply cut a flat reinforcing strip from thick styrene sheet and glue it behind the joint. On walls with windows and doors, you may be able to centre the joint on an aperture and use the moulded window frame or door to align and join the pieces.

Tacking

Because of its free-flowing nature, it is very difficult to stop liquid adhesive from flowing along the length of a joint and

making a permanent bond. But occasionally it may be necessary to make a temporary, deliberately weak, joint which can be easily parted again without damaging the components. This tacking technique, though more common in soldered construction than in working with plastics, can be useful.

To make a tack we need a more viscous adhesive that is more controllable than the liquid. Two candidates are tube cement and Humbrol Precision Poly.

The actual tacking is simplicity itself. Set the components up and support them in position then put little blobs of adhesive at intervals along the joint. If you are using cement, squeeze a little onto a scrap of card or a tin lid and apply the blobs with a cocktail stick. With Precision Poly, you can apply the adhesive straight from the bottle as the fine applicator allows plenty of control. Support the work until the adhesive sets.

Heat techniques

To build a plastic kit as the manufacturer intended rarely requires forming any of the components to shape. But once you start adapting, customising and modifying a kit, you may occasionally need to apply heat to soften plastic parts.

For example, the arced vacuum forming which represents the corrugated iron roof on the coal or builders' merchant [525, 232] and carriage shed [527, 231] kits is ideal for modelling Dutch barns, Nissen huts and a range of other agricultural and industrial buildings. But you may wish to decrease (or, for that matter, increase) the radius of the arc. The easiest way is to curve the roof round a glass bottle, wooden dowel or metal tube of the required diameter, bind it in place with bandage and dunk it in near-boiling water for a few moments. Don't undo the bandage or remove the re-formed roof from its former until it is cold. You can use this technique (and variations on it) for most forming jobs.

Occasionally you may need to form a small bail or knob on the end of a length of styrene microrod. One obvious application would be to produce a cross arm to fit to a lamp post. To do this, you need a small flame – a candle is the best bet.

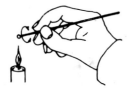

Take a length of microrod between your finger and thumb and rotate it near, or over, the flame for a moment. Hey presto... a globule forms on the end. It takes a few goes to master this so there will be plenty of duds but eventually you'll end up with the perfect size and shape.

A few kits contain etched brass components which may need soldering. Soldering is outside the scope of this book

but a series describing the techniques in verbose detail was published in *Modelling Railways Illustrated, Vol 2, issues 1-7*.

A soldering iron can also be used to 'melt' small metal parts into plastic – door handles, for instance. Be careful to avoid touching the styrene component with the iron because it is difficult to remove melted-on plastic from a bit. Keep an old one specially for this sort of work.

Heat technique safety

The usual method of heating plastic parts in order to form them is to use boiling water. The safety precautions are fairly obvious. Boiling water gives off steam and very hot water vapour which can produce a 'dry scald' and water will scald you long before (or after) it boils. Don't pour boiling or near-boiling water into or onto cold glass containers.

If you already use a soldering iron, you will know how hot it can get. As with any other soldering iron work, keep the iron in a proper stand and watch where you trail the power lead. If you intend to soften plastic with the iron, don't let the bit reach full working temperature and don't let it actually touch the plastic part.

Using tube cement

If the ubiquitous liquid adhesive is the principal medium for assembling plastic kits, what role remains for the good old tube of polystyrene cement? Well, it still has several uses.

Sometimes it is more convenient to apply adhesive to a component before positioning it on the model. For example, if you want to add a small detail to a building, it is often easier to apply a tiny dab of cement and place the component into position with a pair of tweezers. It's possible to soften a component with liquid adhesive and then pop it in place, but it's tricky. If you don't put enough liquid on it will evaporate before you can unite the components. On the other hand, if you use too much, the component will either stick to the tweezers or simply turn into a wilting blob. Cement overcomes this problem.

A fillet of cement along the inside of a joint can often add strength. You can use it by itself or as reinforcement for a joint made with liquid adhesive. It needs to be left overnight to dry but the work can often be planned to accommodate this. In fact, I often beef up joints made with liquid adhesive if they can be left to thoroughly harden.

Cement can be also be diluted to provide a halfway house adhesive, neither too runny nor too viscous. Squeeze a little blob of cement onto a piece of scrap wood or metal (obviously not plastic) then add liquid adhesive, a bit at a time.

The consistency and the setting time can be adjusted easily – more liquid if you want it runny and quick drying, less for a stiffer, slower adhesive. The mixture can be applied by stick or brush and will stay where you put it. It can be useful for tacking and for reinforcing long joints.

When you glaze windows, you will need to stick transparent styrene sheet to the back of the frame or glazing bars. With liquid adhesive, there's always a risk of

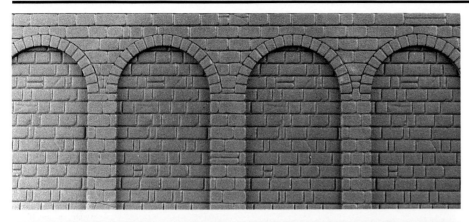

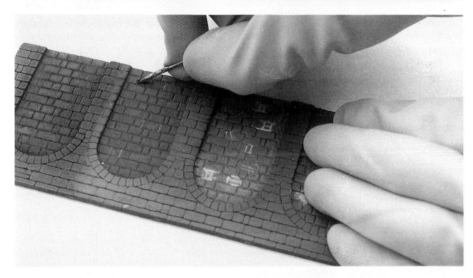

frosting the 'glass'. The more viscous mixture works a treat. It is also ideal if you are adding extra glazing bars made from microrod. Paint a smear of mixture onto the bar then place it with the tweezers.

Although you don't need to laminate sheets of styrene when building kits as intended, you may do once you start to modify them substantially. It is easier to bond the laminate successfully by spreading a fairly thin cocktail of liquid and cement over the mating faces than it is to use either adhesive by itself.

Using cement has certain disadvantages. A joint made with cement will take a lot longer to set than one made with liquid adhesive. But even this drawback can be turned to your advantage sometimes. For instance, it can provide time to adjust the exact position of a component, especially if it must be truly vertical or horizontal.

Another problem with cement is that it can be stringy; in other words, it can produce long sticky filaments. I can't think of a way to exploit this particular weakness but there are several things you can do to minimise stringing.

Firstly, always keep the tube capped, unless you're actually squeezing the glue out. Second, throw partly used tubes away after a couple of months – the older the glue, the more readily it strings in my experience. Third, don't use the tube's nozzle to apply the cement; squeeze a little out and use a bit of wire, a cocktail stick or something similar. But use the glue as soon as you can after decanting it from the tube; the longer it's exposed to the air, the stringier it becomes. Fourth, don't try to separate the components after the glue has been applied. Finally, if you do get a string, perhaps as you withdraw your cocktail stick, try to leave it in place (but clear of the model) until it dries. Then you can pare it away with the scalpel.

Using fillers

If you build a Ratio kit 'straight from the box', you will have very little filling to do because the components are accurately moulded and fit together well. Even so, you won't always get a perfect match and nothing looks worse than a corner with an unwanted split running up it, especially on a wagon or carriage. Use one of the fillers described in Chapter 4 to remedy any such small deficiencies.

It's when you start chopping the kit about or when you want to introduce a bit of variety that fillers come into their own. Quite apart from covering the evidence if you've been a little careless with the fit of your home brewed additions, the filler can

Using filler to modify surface details. In the top photograph, all the arch infills are exactly the same. The second picture shows (from left to right) three stages in the process: the filler applied to cover the characteristic stones, the filler rubbed down, and the mortar courses cleaned out. In the third photograph, the little chisel is being used to gouge out new mortar courses. When the arches are painted, the infills no longer look like peas in a pod, as the last picture shows.

be used to add detail such as flaunching around chimney pots or mortar flashings and so on.

You can also modify surface texture with filler. Take, for example, Ratio's 4mm scale retaining wall [537]. Each section contains four arches and, as you can see from the photograph, the mould for each arch's infill is tooled from the same pattern. Result? The stonework in each arch is the same, cracks and all. This won't look very convincing, especially if you've a long run of retaining wall to install.

This is where the filler comes in. As you will see from the pictures on the previous page, by changing the appearance of just a few stones and altering a few mortar courses, you will introduce sufficient variety to overcome the repetitive regimentation of the infills. The most characteristic 'stones' (and, therefore, the ones that most need altering) are shown in the sketch.

The method is very simple. Dab a spot of filler over each characteristic stone (or whatever other feature you wish to disguise) and let it harden thoroughly. Rub it down flush with the stonework, using wet'n'dry paper supported by a small strip of wood (lolly sticks are good for this) or with an emery board. It's then a simple matter to carve new detail into the filler using your little chisel or gouge. Obviously, you can apply this technique to a wide range of surfaces.

Using the sanding block

There's not a lot to say about this. You can use it to remove surface detail, to thin down mouldings and, by working a component along the edge, to form a step.

The most frequent use of the sanding block, however, is to true up an edge or remove protrusions from it. The trick is to hold the workpiece firmly, draw it across the block rather than saw it to and fro, and not let it rock. This way, you will avoid rounding or sloping the corners, or working a long, convex curve into the edge.

Test the edge for straightness as you go, using your square or steel rule. Like so much else, practice makes perfect so experiment on some offcuts or waste material before you let loose on the kit.

Windows

Although not strictly 'techniques' as such, there are a few things to bear in mind when modelling windows.

The inside corners of moulded window frames will usually benefit from a spot of sharpening up with the scalpel or triangular files as part of the refining process.

The moulded frames are often too thick, front to back, so that the glazing ends up recessed too far into the building. The easiest way round this is to gently rub the whole moulding, inside face downwards, over the sanding block to reduce its overall thickness. This will leave a fluffy rag around the edges that can either be scraped away with a scalpel or burnished off with a glassfibre pencil.

In most cases, it will be a lot easier to paint the frame before it is installed but remember to leave the inside face unpainted so that the adhesive used to fix the glazing will have somewhere to bite.

The clear styrene glazing sheet will mark very easily if excess liquid adhesive runs over it so be very careful. Use a milder brand such as Humbrol Liquid Poly, load the brush very lightly and concentrate on the outside edges rather than trying to make a bond on every glazing bar.

A few of the window frames will be too deep despite your best efforts on the sanding block (those in the concrete platelayers' hut are a case in point) so you may wish to knock replacements up from microstrip and clear styrene.

If you want to model an open window, it's probably easiest to cut out the inside frames and knock up replacements yourself. This is what I did for the hut illustrated in the worked examples.

Finally, if a frame is too thick or the glazing bars look too heavy, you can often substitute items from the various ranges of pre-printed glazing sheets. Freestone Model Accessories stock a lot of these and Exactoscale have an exclusive range as well. It's worth getting hold of their catalogues from the addresses in Appendix 1.

The sanding block is simply a section of flat board with wet'n'dry paper stuck to both sides. Here it's being used to true up an edge. Be careful to keep the workpiece level or the edge will develop a shallow curve.

Chapter Six
EXAMPLES

So far, I have discussed in general terms some of the principles and procedures that will help you get the best from Ratio kits. Now it's time to move from the general to the particular and put the theory into practice.

This chapter explains how the tools, techniques and materials covered earlier are used to assemble, modify and detail a small selection of worked examples. It also shows how to relate Ratio products to their prototypes.

With well over a hundred Ratio models and only a few pages, the selection of examples is inevitably limited. At first sight, it may also appear unrepresentative. But the subjects of the little essays that follow have been chosen because the skills and techniques involved are applicable to most of the other kits in the Ratio range and because each demonstrates the approach outlined in Chapter 2.

In these examples, there are three underlying themes. The first is modelling from the prototype rather than simply following the instructions – all the examples are based on either first hand study or on published photographs. The second is the practical application of the techniques described earlier in this book. The third is the ease with which Ratio kits can be adapted and detailed. Once you decide to model from a prototype, some modification, however minor, is almost always necessary and it is the addition of small details which bring life and authenticity to a model.

A modern image hut

The first worked example is a very simple model, chosen to illustrate modelling from a specific prototype using your own photographs. The subject is Ratio's concrete platelayer's hut [518]. These attractive, chunky little buildings appeared after nationalisation and many still stand today. Although largely confined to the south and west, you also find them further 'up country'.

There are two approaches open to you. You can simply buy the kit, assemble one of the two huts provided in fifteen minutes and follow the recommendation of an overall coat of Humbrol Concrete paint with the doors and windows picked out in green. This will give you a model concrete hut just like everyone else's. Or you can make a model of an actual hut, looking at the Ratio kit as a good starting point.

A mate of mine spotted the hut illustrated in the colour section of this book while we were driving beside the ex-LSWR mainline near Honiton. "Look." he said, "There's a Ratio kit over there." I had my camera with me, so we parked the car and scrambled up the embankment to take a photograph of the hut. The picture, full of detail to capture in model form, is worth studying carefully.

The prototype hut is certainly not a uniform colour. Its warm, greyish beige has a stippled, speckly appearance with a number of light blotches where lichen has died after a long spell of hot and dry weather. There are quite distinct paler streaks below the window and a very noticeable rust stain on the corner of the adjacent pillar.

The hut has obviously not been used for years – at least, not for its intended purpose. This dilapidated condition makes it an ideal subject for a modern image layout. Ivy and brambles have completely colonised the back of it and are getting a strong foothold inside. The door has lost half a plank and stains show where resin is oozing from the knots in the wood. The door's original grey paintwork has almost bleached away, leaving the white lead primer showing through. The windows have both been left propped open, the glass long gone. Their white paint is flaking and the steel frames have started to rust. Incidentally, there was no indication that either the door or the window frames had ever been painted green.

Make two cuts to remove the door. You need to keep the little offcut as it forms the corner post of the building.

To model this neglected scrap of recent railway history, you will have to modify the Ratio kit and knock up a few bits from scrap plastic, microrod and glazing sheet. You'll also need to concoct some greenery using the techniques described by Tony Hill in his book *Simply Scenery*, a companion volume in this series.

As I built this particular model, I kept the photograph on the bench in front of me – short of driving back to Honiton and sitting by the lineside with my modelling box, I can't think of a more convenient check on authenticity. If you are using colour photographs in this way, it's best to work near a window during daylight, especially at the painting stage. However, it's better not to define the painting stage too narrowly – it's often best to paint the model as you go along, rather than as a separate job at the end, as you will read in Chapter 8.

The first thing to do is remove all the components from the sprue, tidy up any protrusions and check the fit of the mating faces. Cast a critical eye over the components and ask yourself how they measure up to the prototype. For instance, Ratio's moulded window frames are too deep – the prototype has light steel frames and

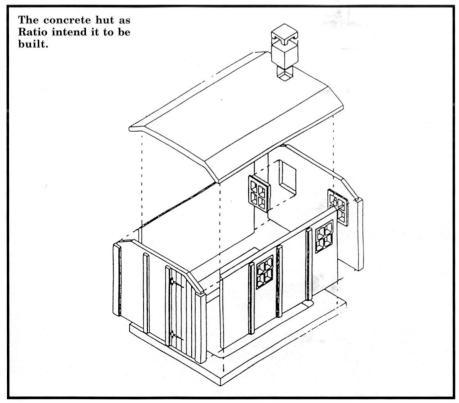

The concrete hut as Ratio intend it to be built.

The classic SR four-panel concrete footbridge. This one, at Woolston, has slightly different piers to the Ratio kits. Photo: John Scrace

the glazing is virtually flush with the outside of the wall. Next, decide what modifications to the components will be necessary. Because the door and window will be modelled open, the moulded door will need to be cut out of the end wall. Use the razor saw for this, cut on the door side of the frames and keep the small square strip from the lower end of the wall as you'll need it for the corner of the building's shell.

As well as adapting the Ratio components, you will need to make some new ones yourself. You'll need a door (the one you cut out will be far too thick and will have no interior detail) and two windows.

Decide a sequence for the work. Once you've cut away the door, you can paint the inside of the roof, walls and base with matt black (or, more accurately, very dark grey) and set them aside to dry while you build the door and windows. If you paint the microstrip for the window frames first, it can be drying while you make the door. Once the door is finished, you may have to leave everything overnight to harden and dry. Then you can assemble the walls and roof. By the time you've painted the door and assembled the windows, the shell of the hut should be strong enough to be painted. Finally, the door and windows can be installed, the vegetation added and the model is ready to set into the layout.

The new door is made of thin styrene sheet. Use the cut-out from the wall of the kit to get the shape, remembering to allow for the width of the two cuts. Cut away a vertical strip halfway up the shorter side of the door to represent the broken plank. Lightly scribe the rest of the planking with the tip of the scalpel or, preferably, a scrawker. Add the internal bracing from microstrip. Finally, add a

The main variant had three panels in the main span, an easy conversion from the Ratio model. This is Rowlands Castle in 1969. Photo: John Scrace

At Pluckley, the bridge has the steps in a 'Z' formation. Photo: John Scrace

latch cut from fine microrod. The smallest size from the assorted pack is about right for this.

The replacement windows are slightly trickier. The method I am going to describe can be used for all sorts of windows in all sorts of models. Begin by drawing the frames actual size in black ink on a sheet of stiff paper, using the Ratio components as templates. Check the drawing against the aperture in the wall, though.

If you want the toplight of the window open, you will need to draw the two frames in each window as separate items. If it's going to be closed, draw them as a single unit. Tape the drawing to your workboard or bench, lay a piece of clear glazing sheet over it and tape that down too.

Select the appropriate size of microstrip from the assorted pack and paint a length of it. For a white frame, painting isn't strictly necessary but it will look better than bare plastic. Once it's dry, lay the end of the microstrip on the glazing sheet, aligning it with an outside frame of the drawing below. Run a little liquid adhesive under the strip from what will be the outside of the frame. As soon as the adhesive bites, nip the excess strip off with the scalpel fairly close to the frame. Carry on in this way until the frame and the glazing bars are all in place. With practice, patience and a mild solvent you should end up with an unblemished window to cut from the glazing sheet.

In some circumstances, you can replace over-thick moulded windows with pre-printed ones which saves a lot of fiddly fabrication. See Appendix 1 for suppliers.

Footbridges

Still with concrete structures, the next worked example demonstrates the adaptability of the larger kits and provides the opportunity for a blow by blow account of a typical constructional sequence. First, though, a brief look at the prototype.

The pre-cast modular footbridge was probably the most successful product of the Exmouth Junction concrete works. It was the first large concrete structure ordered by the newly formed Southern Railway. A good source of prototype information is *Southern Nouveau* by the legendary duo George Reeve and Chris Hawkins (details in Appendix 1).

The footbridge was designed by the Southern's Divisional Engineer W H Shortt. Each bridge was pre-cast as a 'kit' of flat sections that could be rapidly erected on site. Surprisingly, no bolts or other fastenings were required because these footbridges were self-supporting once assembled. They just *sat* there.

The Ratio footbridge kits **[517, 222]** follow the prototype's construction. For instance, the prototype piers are, to quote Shortt, 'firmly held together by the landing slabs which are made in the form of caps'. This is also how the model is arranged – hardly surprising, as Ratio designed the kit from the plans and description in *Southern Nouveau*.

There were two main variations of the standard footbridge; the pattern with four

Eynsford's footbridge was unusual in the way the steps doubled back on themselves. Photo: John Scrace

I built this 4mm scale model of the Eynsford footbridge to demonstrate the adaptability of the Ratio kit.

panels in the main span and the shorter three-panel version. Ratio's model depicts the four-panel type.

The four-panel bridge was the most common sort and dozens could be found throughout south and west England. There were a few in South Wales too. By the 1930s, the use of these bridges was

widespread and they were still being erected as recently as the early 1960s. Many of them are still in use.

Variations abounded. The bridge at Woldingham was fitted with a roof and windowed sides – today, the sides are open but the roof remains. At Eynsford, Kent, the bridge was asymmetrical. The

Woodmansterne station boasted a real hybrid footbridge as described in the text. My 2mm scale model was built from a photograph published in a Middleton Press album.

flight of steps at one end was at a right angle to the main span but at the other end the steps were in line with it. To fit the location, these in-line steps doubled back on themselves and had an extra landing, as shown in the photograph. Wateringbury station had staggered platforms. To link them, the footbridge had its two flights of steps facing opposite ways to give a 'Z' formation.

A real hybrid graced Woodmansterne station. Its footbridge not only provided access to the single island platform but also linked housing estates on either side of the line. Two three-panel sections spanned the tracks and were supported by a central pier from which a flight of steps with an intermediate landing led to the platform. This central flight faced east, the single flight at the north end of the bridge faced west and at the south end, the flight was in line with the main span and had an intermediate landing and pier.

Usually, however, three-panel bridges only differed from the four-panel type in respect of the main span. The flights of steps and the landings were common to both.

Although mainly found at stations, three-panel bridges were also used to carry local footpaths over open line. In this situation, the bridge had to rise from track level, rather than from platform height, so it had two flights of steps at each side rather than the usual single ones. The flights were separated by an intermediate landing. There is a good photograph of this type of bridge in *Southern Nouveau*.

The modular design of the prototype lent itself to simple linear extension. The main span of the Exeter Central foot-

The concrete footbridge (model and prototype) can be extended, like this example at Coulsdon North. Photo: John Scrace

Perhaps the best known of the extended concrete footbridges spanned Seaton Junction station. This 1949 view shows the four-panel and six-panel spans and cross-braced piers. An Adams Radial 4-4-2T and M7 0-4-4T have just arrived with a Seaton-Waterloo service. Photo: S C Nash

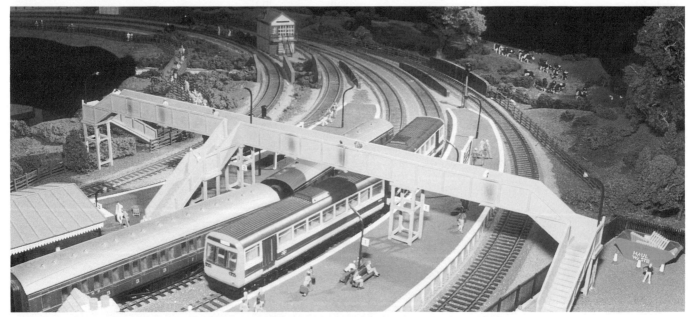

A scene on Pecorama's Loft Layout. This extended Ratio footbridge was inspired by the Seaton Junction prototype. Behind it is Ratio's GWR signal box. Photo: courtesy of Peco Studios

bridge swept across two platform roads and two through roads. At Seaton Junction an even longer example extended right across the station. These longer footbridges were supported on pairs of heavy cross-braced columns rather than the lighter four column type in the Ratio kit. A standard kit is illustrated on the cover

but, like their prototypes, Ratio's footbridge components are very adaptable.

A good example of this is the extended bridge, inspired by Seaton Junction, which features on Peco's 'Loft Layout'. This layout – and many more – can be viewed at Peco's excellent permanent model railway exhibition and visitor centre,

Pecorama (for further details, see Appendix 1).

Many of the possible conversions of the Ratio footbridge will require extra components as well as a complete kit. The mouldings are available separately from Ratio. You can order them by post (telephone for prices), collect them from the factory or buy them from the firm's exhibition stand.

One problem with kitbashing the bridge is that many of the components are handed. For instance, the two sides of the main steps are different lengths. And if you want different configurations of the landings, you will probably have to knock up alternative sides from styrene sheet and microstrip.

The simplest conversion of the Ratio bridge is to the type with the three-panel main span. Assuming you intend to retain the standard arrangement of piers and steps, this doesn't require any extra mouldings and you won't have to fabricate any additional bits. I will describe the conversion a little further on.

Before that, though, here are a few notes on assembling a standard four-panel bridge 'out of the box'. Most of the remarks apply to the 4mm scale model but the procedure is similar in 2mm scale.

A typical 'out of the box' Ratio footbridge pictured at an exhibition (although I can't remember which one).

Careful preparation of the components is, as always, the prerequisite of a good model. The components of the bridge kits (particularly the 4mm scale one) have a rash of extraction pips around the edges.

After cutting off the pips, the outside edges can be smoothed on the sanding block. The inside edges (such as those within the pier sections) will need some deft scraping with the scalpel. This calls for a light touch in the case of the 2mm scale kit.

Although there are no written instructions, the exploded diagram clearly shows where the components locate. Construct the bridge as several sub-assemblies, allowing the adhesive plenty of time to harden at each stage before moving on to the next. It's best to leave the sub-assemblies overnight before uniting them.

There are a few traps for the unwary. Make sure the steps are the right way up by checking the treads and the risers (it is possible to assemble the model with the steps upside down). As with any other plastic kit, have a dry run before you commit yourself with the adhesive.

To build the 4mm scale bridge, I find the following order of assembly is easiest. The first job, if you want to add handrails as described later, is to make and fit them to the two main spans.

With the handrails done (or not, as the case may be), take the deck section and centre it lengthways on the inside of one span. It locates on the moulded rebate, *not* on the pips below. On the 2mm scale model, you are denied the luxury of a location rebate; assemble the deck so that the underside is flush with the bottom of the main spans. In both scales, the textured side of the deck goes uppermost.

Now you need a sheet of glass or truly flat board and your square. Check that the deck and the span are square to one another and run a brushload of liquid adhesive along the joint from underneath the bridge. Add the second span. Before the adhesive fully hardens, check that the two spans are parallel in end elevation and square to the deck so that the assembly rests on your flat surface without rocking. When this spans-and-deck unit is dry, add the two short lengths of steps. They may need thinning slightly on the sanding block to drop snugly between the spans. Set this sub-assembly aside to harden thoroughly.

Build the two piers as shown in the drawing, again checking that the assembly is square and will stand without rocking. Cap each pier with a landing and set aside to dry.

When the pier-and-landing units are hard, add the pairs of sides that enclose the longer steps (having first installed handrails if you want them). These sides are handed – the longer one of each pair (which also has a longer cut-out in the bottom web) goes on the outside of the bridge (that is, furthest from the span). The moulded slots in the landing help identify the correct position. You may also find that a dry run with the span, piers and side sections will help to clarify things, although it should be obvious from the drawing. Once you're sure you've got it right, position the longer steps, making sure they meet the landing at the top and the ground at the bottom. Tack the assembly together from above with a few tiny drops of adhesive, let it harden then carefully invert the assembly and run a brushload of adhesive along the joint from below.

All that remains is to unite the span and pier assemblies and add the sides of the landings, fettling them for a good, close fit. A peg is moulded on two of these landing sides (one at either end of the bridge) which locates into the square hole in the landing. Note that the other pair of landing sides (or, more properly, backs) have one angled edge; this is the top edge and slopes down from the main span towards the outside of the bridge.

Now for the three-panel version. Converting the main span involves removing a panel from each of the two sides and shortening the deck. This is a good exercise in accurate cutting.

First, make two cuts across each span with a razor saw, as shown in the photograph (you may care to revisit the notes on razor sawing in Chapter 5). Cut next to the moulded uprights so that you won't have a joint showing in the middle of a panel. Be very careful to get the cuts dead square. If you keep the saw vertical, the joint on the inside of the span should be a close enough fit to need no filler.

Once you've done all the cutting, butt the mating halves of each main span together and check that both the spans will be exactly the same length when the pairs are re-united. Align the two halves of the span accurately, then run solvent into the joint from what will be the inside of each span. Leave them overnight to harden,

Construct the footbridge kits as sub assemblies, as in these 2mm and 4mm scale four-panel examples.

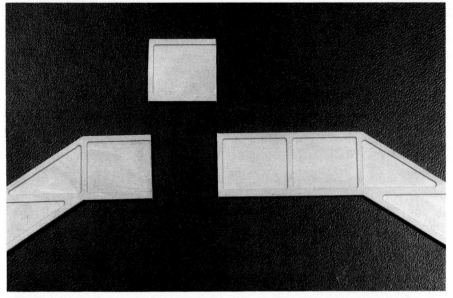

Make two razor saw cuts to produce a three-panel main span. The cuts are close up to the moulded framing.

Fitting a 0.45mm brass wire handrail into drilled blind holes. A drop of liquid adhesive is enough to secure the rail.

then smooth the faces on the sanding block.

To shorten the deck, only one cut is necessary. Use one of the shortened spans to ascertain how much needs to be removed. The ends of the deck should line up with the points where the moulded rebate changes angle at the top of the steps. Cut the excess length from one end of the deck. Again, be very careful to get the cut dead square and to keep the saw vertical. The

and forego the intermediate brackets.

For the 4mm scale model, microrod is too fragile for the handrails. Use 0.45mm straight brass wire from Alan Gibson (see Appendix 1 for the address). This is virtually scale size. In 2mm scale, on the other hand, separate wire handrails standing out from the sides would be very fiddly and delicate and it is far easier to make them from microrod stuck directly to the bridge with liquid adhesive.

you, I have only seen one photograph of a bridge fitted with them.

The other optional components are the two smoke deflectors. These were seldom fitted to bridges on Southern electrified lines and many were removed when steam traction finished elsewhere. If you fit them, make sure they are directly above the track centreline(s).

Grounded carriages and vans

The next example shows how detail can bring a model to life. The subject is a bit hard to track down nowadays, so rather than getting out with the camera you will probably have to work from published sources. Magazines and books often contain photographs of old carriage and van bodies put to other uses. Such pictures can provide the inspiration for an interesting model; the selection here should give you some ideas. You'll find some of the features reproduced in the worked example.

Because railway carriages and vans were built to last from high quality materials, their bodywork was often still intact when higher standards overtook them, new stock superseded them or their running gear became too old to be economically repaired. The railway companies often gave a second lease of life to old vehicles as sheds, staff mess huts and store-rooms. These were most commonly found at freight yards, works, major stations and locomotive depots, although many smaller stations also hosted them.

Some rolling stock bodies, particularly vans, were sold off by the railway company and many are to be seen to this day in farm yards and around industrial premises. Carriage bodies in non-railway locations are rarer, although a few did end up as summer houses, chalets and so on. Ken Northwood (whose influential 00 gauge *North Devonshire Railway* was featured in *Modelling Railways Illustrated, Vol 2 No 9*) modelled just such a chalet, using two Ratio grounded carriage kits **[501]**. There is a photograph of it in the colour section.

Ratio produces three kits for grounded bodies. The grounded van **[507]** uses the body of the SR 12T Ventilated Van kit and the two grounded carriages are the little GWR composite **[501]** and the Midland Rly All Third/Luggage **[519]**. However, many of the other vehicles from the

The completed three-panel span with handrails installed. You can just see the joint line on the inside face of the wall. In front of the bridge are the lamps referred to in the text.

rest of the assembly work is as described above for the standard bridge.

Handrails are quite noticeable in photographs of the prototype but are not provided in Ratio's footbridge kits. The omission is very easy to remedy. The rails run down both sides of each flight of steps, including the short flights in the main span. Some footbridges have them round the landings as well.

The handrails are supported on underslung brackets. There is one at each end of the rail and one, two or three intermediate ones. On a model, however, it is easier to simply turn the ends inwards

To attach the wire handrails, you can either melt them into the bridge sides with a soldering iron or stick them into pre-drilled blind holes. In either case, be careful not to break through to the outside of the bridge.

Finally, the last few details. There is a little post moulded onto each of the two 'pegged' landing sides to carry the lamps supplied with the kit. The lamps themselves are made up from three components; a stepped base, a solid lamp body and a pyramid roof. Ratio also provides glazing sheet so that you can make up 'see through' lamps if you wish to. Mind

A classic example of a grounded carriage body. This inspired the little scene illustrated in the colour pages.

An even more decrepit carriage body was used as a bike shed and mess room at Three Bridges locomotive depot. This photograph gave me the idea for the open door and skeletal panelling on the model.

range would do as well, if you're willing to consign the underframe to the scrapbox. The model in this example is based on kit [501]. The moulded carriage sides and ends are the same as for the carriage kit proper [612], so they include both the door and grab handles. Grab handles were usually cast in brass and were retrieved before the carriage was condemned, so carefully pare them away with the little chisel, along with the door handles. You can drill small holes at the door handle locations to suggest that the handle, its surrounding escutcheon and the lock have been removed.

Many grounded carriages were removed from their metal underframes. The three prototypes illustrated here, for example, are sitting directly on their floors. The Ratio carriage has the headstocks (which are part of the underframe) moulded integrally with the ends. Cut them from the ends with the razor saw or Stanley knife.

You can 'plank' some of the windows over, a bit of a modelling cliché but authentic for all that. There are individual boards on one of the mouldings supplied with the kit, but they are rather hefty for this application so cut replacements from very thin styrene strip or sheet.

You may wish to model the grounded carriage with a door (or doors) either stood open or boarded over from the inside. If you look at the photographs, you will see that the door frames (and other internal vertical framing) taper below the waist to produce the characteristic turn-under (often mis-termed 'tumblehome') of the carriage sides. The door itself is also thinner at the bottom.

The Ratio moulded sides, however, are a uniform thickness from top to bottom and will need thinning to the profile shown in the sketch below.

Start by cutting out a door with the razor saw, following the two moulded lines

Remove the shaded area adjacent to the doors.

on the sides. Be sure that the waste side of the cut falls in the door opening, rather than the carriage side. This, of course, means that the door, once cut out, will be too narrow. You can either live with the inaccuracy or make a full-width replacement door out of styrene sheet. The new door need only be detailed on the inside as the outer face will be swung against the carriage side, as the photographs make clear.

The two separated sections of carriage side need tapering immediately adjacent to the door. The easiest way is to rub the sides on the edge of the sanding block as shown on the sketch. It's not necessary to treat more than a few millimetres either side of the doorway. This leaves the moulded location flange along most of the side.

To model a boarded-up door, simply re-unite the sections of side with a piece of

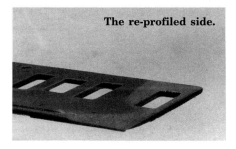

The re-profiled side.

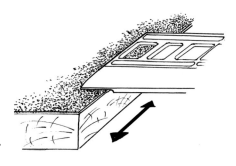

Reducing the thickness on the edge of the sanding block.

styrene sheet, distressed to represent the wood grain. Because the real door opened from *under* the top line of panelling, you will need to splice in a little offcut as shown in the photographs. The floor will also need a little strip adding so that it extends out to meet the thinned-down side.

For an open door, assemble the two sections of side to the carriage floor, taking

Even if you're not modelling the interior, fill the holes and scribe the floor to represent planking around the open door. The little fillet of styrene extends the floor to full width in the doorway.

Neatly arrayed tools like these can add a sense of purpose to your model mess hut or stores.

care to get them aligned. Splice in the offcuts to continue the panelling above the door opening and to extend the floor. Paint the model before finally hanging the door. When you add the glazing to the sides, try not to let the edge of the clear sheet show through the open door.

You can employ similar procedures if you fancy modelling a section of side with the lower panelling missing, as shown in the photographs. It's a fiddly job, but the resulting skeletal look is very satisfying.

With an open door, it will be possible to see into the carriage. You may not fancy having a go at a full interior but you should at least fill the more obvious holes in the floor and texture it to suggest planking. You may wish to add the bulkheads between the compartments, both to add rigidity and so that not too many windows on the far side show through the open door. That said, quite often several bulkheads

would have been removed on the prototype.

The roof is another area where you can individualise the model. As the photographs show, roofs often suffered and were patched up with roofing felt or an old tarpaulin held down with planks and a brick.

To cover a roof in 'felt', first pare away the ventilators and scrape off the rain strips. This needn't be done very painstakingly as the actual surface will be hidden. Rub the roof surface smooth with wet'n'dry. Now take some toilet tissue, the soft type. This is almost always two ply – separate the layers, as you will only need a single thickness.

The next stage uses quite a lot of liquid adhesive, so open the windows or decamp into the garden. Load a largish paintbrush with adhesive and flood the tissue paper, making sure that it lays flat to the roof. The adhesive will soak through and bond the tissue to the plastic, leaving a suitably textured surface.

The paint used on the roof will have to be thinned down a lot, partly because the surface is absorbent and partly to avoid clogging the texture. One solution is to colour the roof as you stick the tissue down. Pick up a splodge of matt black paint on the adhesive brush, work the excess onto a piece of cloth then load the brush with adhesive. As the liquid soaks over the roof tissue, the diluted black will run with it, staining the white tissue

a dirty grey colour. You may have to experiment a bit on some scrap styrene sheet to get an even colour.

Ratio supplies a stovepipe for the grounded carriages. You can use this, but if you want a taller chimney, simply substitute a length of plastic rod or Fineline Styrene tube. Don't position it in the middle of the roof; usually the stove was near the side or end of the vehicle, away from the door out of harm's way. Don't forget a little heap of coal near the door and perhaps a pile of kindling.

Junk and clutter

Old carriage and van bodies lead us naturally to the junk and clutter which often surrounded them. This sort of detailing is great fun to do and can add a great deal of life and interest to a layout. Don't overdo it though. Real railways were seldom in a state of chaotic untidiness. To get a feel for authenticity, spend some time studying books, magazines and photographic albums.

To represent junk and clutter, we can press almost anything into service. Sewing thread can be coiled and hung on shed walls to represent ropes. Sections of waste sprue, especially the thicker variety, can easily be squared up on the sanding block and cut to length as timber baulks and packing blocks, a moment's work with the scrawker or scalpel imparting the wood grain.

The various smaller angles, 'L' and 'H' sections in the Fineline Styrene range can be used to represent scrap angle iron and lengths of rolled steel joist. Planks and boards of all shapes and sizes can be cut from Microstrip. Small squares of thin styrene sheet can represent offcuts of plywood. Ratio's vacuum-formed corrugated roofing, supplied with kits **[232, 231, 317, 525 and 527]**, can be cut up into individual sheets and stacked up or stood against walls.

Ladders and steps were often found around yards and short ones are included in Ratio's grounded carriage body kits. In 2mm scale, kit **[218]** contains a generous ten inches of ladder which can be cut into suitable lengths; the 4mm scale equiva-

If you want to model a full interior, this view of loco crews relaxing at Redhill just after the war will help you. Photo: N I Binns

The completed 4mm scale model, incorporating features from all the prototypes illustrated in this chapter. A view of the model in its setting is included in the colour pages.

Modelling clutter is very satisfying. The fencing, 45-gallon drums, pallets, ladder and chair are Ratio mouldings, the wheelbarrow and spade are from Coopercraft, the timber baulks and assorted other bits are made from sprue or microstrip. I can't remember the provenance of the van body. The scenic treatments are as described in Tony Hill's *Simply Scenery*.

24 oil drums. There are other useful items for this sort of detailing on the individual sprues that are available direct from Ratio. The main sprue of the yard crane kit [531] includes a winding drum and gear wheels, while the base sprue of the GWR signal box [500] has a 45-gallon oil drum with a wooden trestle to stand it on. The grounded carriage body kits contain a sprue of sleepers, timber battens, a 45-gallon oil drum, a short ladder, a planked table and two tiny chairs.

Tools were often left outside mess rooms and huts and often a wheelbarrow would be stood against a wall, nose down to keep the rain from filling it.

Coopercraft produce a useful set of plastic mouldings to represent these items.

One modelling cliché to avoid is the heap of locomotive or wagon wheels dotted about, usually as a result of motorising Airfix kits, re-wheeling RTR engines or substituting metal wagon wheels for plastic ones.

Other rolling stock components were more commonly seen, however. Three link and screw couplings turned up in odd places, often hanging on walls. Brake blocks might be found stacked up as well.

If you're modelling a modern preserved railway, you can get away with much more. Tender bodies, cabs, boilers, driving wheels, buffers and so on can all be seen at relatively small preserved stations.

With a little lateral thinking and ingenuity, most of the junk, clutter and odds and sods that add so much character to the railway scene can be recreated.

Telegraph poles

Ratio's pack of telegraph poles [452] provides an example of how a simple one-piece moulding can be easily modified to provide a lot of variations.

The railway companies were the first major users of the electric telegraph. The line of telegraph poles linking stations and signal boxes alongside the tracks be-

lent is the pack of signal ladders [451], a total of twenty-four inches. Folding step ladders can be knocked up from microstrip, although it's a fiddly business, especially in 2mm scale.

The components in kit [419] offer a lot of detailing possibilities. The concrete posts can be stacked up and the notice boards leant against a shed wall. The water standpipes with taps can be sited around yards or just outside mess huts. The kit even includes some very rural 'clutter' – a selection of cow pats.

Wooden pallets and 45-gallon oil drums often appear in the most unlikely places – nowadays the whole country seems to be over-run by pallets. So kit [514] will always find a home. It contains four drums, six pallets and thirty sacks in 4mm scale. Additional 4mm scale sacks are available as [426]. In 2mm scale, kit [221] contains ten pallets, 42 sacks and

Photographs of junk and clutter can provide inspiration for hours of detail modelling. Timber baulks, re-railing wedges, packing crates, a 45-gallon drum, an old lorry wheel... and that's before you start looking at the hut or carriage body.

Now that's what I call a telegraph pole! Over forty feet of pine, fifteen cross arms and 60-odd insulators, towering over Bulleid Pacific 34091 at Yeovil Junction.

Close up of a prototype photographed beside the Severn Valley Railway. This may not be as impressive as the Yeovil Junction example, but it's more typical of secondary lines and easily modelled with Ratio's mouldings.

Here's something I've never seen modelled - a linesman working up a pole. The lower, staggered metal footholds are called 'pole steps' by the men; the upper pair on which they work are 'standing steps'.

came one of the most characteristic elements of the steam age railway. Today, ground conduits, radio telephony and microwave transmission mean the poles have largely vanished from the railway scene, leaving you to fall back on published photographs for prototype information.

Telegraph poles varied enormously. Their height could range from under 20ft (about three inches in 4mm scale) to over 50ft although the average was 30ft. The poles themselves were usually the trunks of pines and consequently tapered slightly from bottom to top. To inhibit rotting, they were soaked in creosote or gas tar. At the top of the pole, the end grain of the wood needed protecting from the ingress of rain water so the pole was cut with a shallow 'A' rather than being cut off square. More often than not, it would also be capped with a little 'roof' of galvanised steel sheet, the bottom edge of which could be either cut off square or rounded.

The wires were carried by insulators mounted on cross arms. These varied from a single arm near the top of the pole to a dozen, the lowest of which might be less than halfway up. Each arm could carry two, four or more insulators. The more insulators, the longer the arms because the wires had to be kept a certain distance apart. As always, you should study published photographs in railway books and in magazines – with telegraph poles, there is certainly no shortage of reference material.

The siting of the poles is important. On open stretches of line, poles were very

seldom more than seventy yards apart and usually a lot less. The spacing, which varied from company to company, was a compromise between the minimum expenditure on poles and the need to adequately support and separate the wires. The GWR, for instance, standardised on 32 poles to the mile. Translated into 4mm scale, this gives a spacing of just over two feet.

In stations, yards, congested urban areas and where the line curved, the spacing of poles would be closer and if the line of wires spanned a railway, a road or a bridge, the adjacent poles would be as close to one another as practical. As a rule, a line of poles would be routed on the inside of curves so that if one fell, the pull of the wires would topple it away from the running lines.

On small layouts, a common fault is too many poles crammed into too short a space. Conversely, a larger model railway may have them spaced too thinly. But an even more jarring sight is a line of model telegraph poles that are not vertical, or at least parallel. They really leap out at you.

This is a paradox, because real telegraph poles often leaned over alarmingly as they settled, as you can see from even a cursory study of published photographs. They were frequently neither vertical nor parallel with one another. Yet, nine times out of ten, reproducing this effect in model form will simply fail to look convincing. On the other hand, telegraph poles beside the great main lines often receded into the distance as straight as soldiers on parade. So, unless you are modelling a specific prototype location to the last detail, it is probably safer to make sure that all your poles are truly vertical.

Quite often, the wires linking a particular building to the main run of poles would be supported on intermediate insulators mounted on other suitable structures such as lamp posts. Where the wires terminated at their destination, there would also be a pair of insulators. Again, a glance through albums will provide lots of prototype examples to model.

Regulations prescribed minimum heights for the wire; 20ft over a main road or 17ft over a railway, for instance. The actual length of pole used depended on the location. As an example, those found in cuttings might be shorter than those beside embankments and taller poles would be employed to raise the wires above roads, bridges or other features. Consult your photographs for examples.

Ratio's 4mm scale kit provides sixteen 40ft poles (enough, at a 2ft spacing, to equip 32ft of layout), each with four cross arms. They are moulded in black styrene and represent the type of pole typically found on secondary routes and branches.

Having carefully parted the individual poles from their runners, use the scalpel or craft knife to scrape off the mould partline that runs down either side of the pole, finishing off with fine wet'n'dry paper. Run the paper up and down the pole rather than round it; any scratches that are left will give the effect of grain. There is a runner between each pole, about halfway

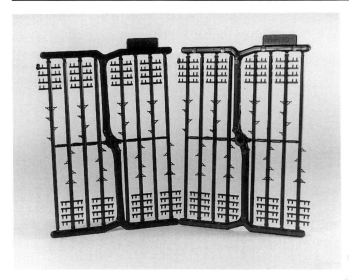

In 4mm scale, Ratio give you sixteen poles on two sprues. Only two of the insulators have a halo of flash - not bad out of 256.

CUT OFF RUNNER THEN SMOOTH THE FLATS OF THE CAP WITH A FINE FILE OR ABRASIVE PAPER

PARE FLASH AWAY

SQUARE UP TAPER

SCRAPE OFF MOULD PART-LINE THEN SMOOTH WITH FINE ABRASIVE PAPER

Preparing Ratio telegraph poles is mainly a matter of overcoming the exigencies of the manufacturing process.

A few cuts with the scalpel will transform the poles.

REMOVE SHADED AREAS – USE TWO CUTS TO PRODUCE ANGLE AT TOP OF POST

ADD CAP OF FOLDED PAPER

down; take particular care here or you will be left with a noticeable bump in the pole.

Another runner protrudes from the moulded protective cap atop the pole. Be careful to preserve the angled flats of the cap as you cut the pole free. The flats may need a touch on the sanding block to finish them off neatly. It's also worth carefully reducing the slight release taper on the cross arms by scraping.

Modifying the poles is easy. The most obvious way is simply to remove an insulator or two – a glance at prototype photographs will show how common this was. If you want fewer cross arms, it is simpler to remove the upper ones by cutting through the pole than to try and pare lower ones away. Make two cuts as shown in the diagram to preserve the angled cut of the prototype and make a new cap from thin stiff paper. Cut several 3mm wide strips, fold them end to end and then trim them off a couple of millimetres from the fold to produce the caps. Place these on the angled top of the poles and secure them with a drop of liquid adhesive, which will readily soak through the paper.

If you need more than four cross arms, the easiest way is to sacrifice a pole; in other words, use two to make one. In one of the worked examples, I have opted for eight arms but obviously you can add as many as you like using this method. More than eight will mean sacrificing another pole. It would be pushing things to go above a dozen. Poles with more arms than this

In the centre, a standard Ratio telegraph pole flanked by reduced and extended versions. Why have yours looking like everyone else's when they're so easy to convert?

were usually only seen beside main lines and were likely to be much thicker than the Ratio ones. Sometimes multiple arms needed a pair of poles, arranged in an 'A' or 'H' formation.

To add cross arms, prepare your 'base' pole then remove the cap from the top of the post, taking care to get the cut square. Then cut the required number of cross arms from the top of the sacrificial pole, leaving the cap in place. Again, make sure the cut is square. Try the two bits together to check that the cross arms are evenly spaced, trimming carefully until they are.

Apply a drop of liquid adhesive to each cut end, repeating until the plastic is softened then press the two components together. If the cuts are accurate, there

The glazed ceramic insulators were usually either a light cream or rich brown colour when new. The gloss soon dulled and, in steam days, the effects of soot and dirt subdued the colours. A touch of greyish buff paint will make the insulators stand out a bit, but not too much. Don't use unadulterated white.

The metal caps were often galvanised, best represented with a touch of dull grey. The footsteps can be picked out in the same

These photographs show the diversity of lamps that can be fitted to Ratio's concrete post.

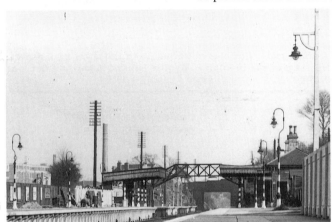

should be no gap and a tiny raised bead of plastic will be squeezed out around the joint. This can smoothed off later.

Eye the pole from all angles and tweak the top until the two lengths of pole are as straight as you can get them. When the plastic has fully rehardened, smooth the joint carefully.

The height of the pole is simply adjusted by cutting the required amount off the bottom or splicing in a length of sacrificial pole. If the pole is shortened, you may wish to remove one or more of the footsteps. Similarly, by sacrificing a pole, extra footsteps can be added to taller poles.

Incidentally, the top pair of footsteps are level with each other while the rest are staggered up the pole. Don't be tempted to remove one of the top pair. They are for the linesman to stand on as he works, as the photograph shows.

The colour of telegraph poles varied and, of course, they were never shiny, unlike the styrene from which the model poles are moulded. So even used straight from the pack, the poles will need painting. If you have modified the poles, the paint will help disguise the surgery. A newly installed telegraph pole was a rich tarry brown but this soon weathered to a lighter dull brown, eventually ageing to a fairly pale grey.

SOME OF THE LAMPS CARRIED ON CONCRETE POSTS (NOT TO SCALE)

colour if you're modelling a newly installed pole, or simply painted in with the main colour.

Lamps

In this last brief example, a little crosskitting and a raid on the scrapbox will enable you to model a wide variety of lamps. Even here, there is a concrete flavour - one of the most popular Ratio lineside accessories is the elegant Exmouth Junction pre-cast lamp post.

The earliest LSWR cast concrete station lamp post was octagonal in section with a heavy base and an ornate finial cast on top. The Ratio model **[454]** represents the later Southern version with a plainer tapering square section. This type was installed by the thousand on stations from Kent to Cornwall.

The older posts were usually equipped with lamps featuring an elegant hexagonal shade made up from individual panes of glass with leaded joints. Later, this became a one-piece hexagonal shade. The lamp itself could be either a gas mantle or electric bulb.

Other types of lamp were often fitted to these posts – in fact, the Southern's much vaunted 'standard' station lamps were anything but. The most common types are shown in the sketch, and the photographs give an idea of the variety to be seen.

The open-ended half-round 'hood' type is simple to model with a curved piece of card, thin styrene sheet, brass shim or section of metal or plastic tube. Modelling the more elaborate, 'old fashioned'

type of gas lamp is also easy using components from Ratio's swan-neck lamps **[453]**, lengths of microrod and small glass beads as shown in the diagram.

The flat dished metal shade is a bit more difficult to reproduce. Crosskitting provided the solution shown in the photograph, the main part of the shade being the lamp body from the swan-neck lamp. There is a blind hole moulded in the top of this component. Drill this through with a 0.7mm drill bit then cut the top section of the lamp body away as shown in the diagram and smooth the cut edge with fine wet'n'dry. For the neck of the shade, use the tapered stem from a hexagonal shade **[454]**. Before cutting it off, carefully drill a 0.7mm hole through the centre. The various bits can then be united

with a length of microrod and the bulb represented by cutting the tip from one of the translucent 'lenses' from kit **[453]**.

If you are installing several posts on a station, select one style of lamp to equip all of them. A mix of types will be noticeable and, being unusual on the prototype, will be unconvincing on the model. That said, there are plenty of exceptions to the rule. The photograph taken at Crayford station in 1955 shows a row of cast iron swan-neck posts and a solitary concrete one.

The Ratio concrete posts need a little preparation. Cut the runner where it joins the sprue, leaving a spigot to mount the post into a pre-drilled hole. There are extraction pips above each arm to be cut off. Remove the prominent part-line by rubbing the flat faces of the post on the sanding block. Obviously you can only use this

technique on the straight sides of the posts; scrape with the scalpel and finish with either fine wet'n'dry or a file around the curved brackets and arms. Square these up and make sure the inside corners are nice and crisp.

The shades are moulded with a single feed to their runners. If you cut close with a really sharp blade, they need no further preparation. To attach them, it is easier to set the posts upside down (either by holding them in the vice or pushing the tops into a block of balsa wood) and add the inverted shades from above. If you've painted the lamps and posts before assembling them, use a tiny drop of cement applied with a pin. If you use liquid adhesive, you risk stripping the paint or marking the shade.

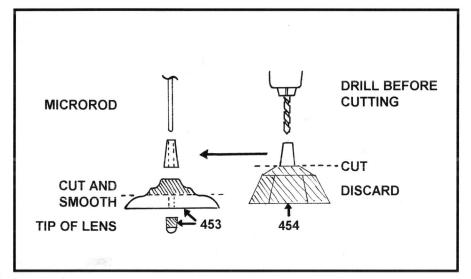

The posts are moulded with two arms; generally only those on island platforms retained both. It is a moment's work to cut off an arm if required, rubbing the face of the post on the sanding block afterwards to hide the scars.

The posts were usually along the centreline of island platforms and along the back of single faced ones, but there were exceptions. They were almost always set so that the arms faced across the platform but occasionally they faced along it. No doubt the SR's engineers specified a standard spacing for the lamps (although I can find no record of it); photographic evidence suggests that it varied from one location to another. About 50ft seems average, so if you space the 4mm scale posts at eight inch intervals along your platform they should look right. Paint the posts before adding the lamp itself or any

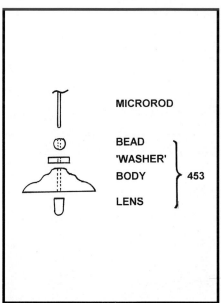

A selection of the lamps described in the text displayed on Ratio concrete poles.

You can make a variety of swan-neck lamps from Ratio's kit [453]. The tallest one also incorporates some brass wire and a glass bead.

The 2mm scale lamp [213].

other details. Leave the hexagonal shade unpainted because the sheen of the plastic gives a convincing pearl glass effect. Pick out the neck of the shade as it was a metal fitting which was painted. If you want to represent the earlier leaded pattern of hexagonal shade, carefully draw along each edge of the Ratio component between the panes with a very fine pen. The other types of shade were made of metal and so were painted. They could be white, cream, or green according to location.

Moving away from concrete, Ratio produces various other types of lamp. In 2mm scale, kit [213] contains four lamps complete with ladders. These are suitable for street lights, stations and yards; they are also included in the 2mm scale cattle dock kit [202]. The posts are flat-sided and the lamp has a pyramid cap and optional finial. The post is fairly short (assembled with the finial, the lamps are a scale equivalent of about 15ft high).

In 4mm scale, I have already mentioned the swan-neck lamps [453]. I find this kit particularly useful because the individual components are so useful for crosskitting. The pack contains enough components for up to nine lamps on posts. They can be assembled in many ways using just the components supplied in the kit, but with a bit of ingenuity, microrod, microstrip, and oddments from the scrapbox, you can make an even greater variety. For instance, the tall lamp post on the left of the photograph was made from two posts grafted together with an alternative shape of swan-neck made from brass wire.

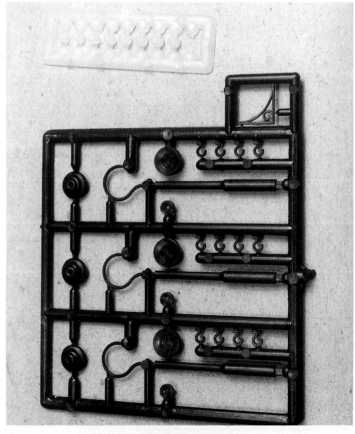

What you get in the swan-neck lamp pack.

Chapter Seven
RATIO SIGNALS
By Mike Romans

Old and new signalling at Banbury in 1993. The GWR semaphore stop signals can be modelled using Ratio products. Photo: Tony Wright

covering the GWR, LNWR, LNER, and LMS in 4mm scale and the LMS (straight post signals only) and GWR in 2mm scale. Most of the 4mm kits allow the construction of simple bracket and splitting signals but for GWR fans such variety is only offered by the kit portraying signals with a square timber post.

A second 4mm scale GWR kit covers the tubular steel style but this does not cater for bracketed signals. This category also includes a kit for the LMS Pratt Truss style of gantry. Available in both 4mm and 2mm scales, this is suitable, as supplied, for spanning two tracks.

The ready-to-assemble kits

The ready-to-assemble range, although limited, has a number of plus points, particularly the pre-coloured arms and glazed spectacle plates. The disadvantage is that there is a fairly small range of signal formations. By the time you've modified them, you might just as well have started with a kit from the first category.

Despite this lack of flexibility, these particular kits enable you to produce some nice looking signals quickly. They also cover the basic requirements well enough to serve the modeller of any of the post-grouping railways, especially in the case of simple track layouts.

The GWR timber post type can be adapted by using etched arms from other manufacturers to approximate the style of some other pre-grouping railway companies. Some modellers have modified the GWR bracket kit to slightly different bracket forms, a three doll version being

Ratio has been producing model signals in plastic since 1963. The original products depicted GWR prototypes and came as fully assembled signals. The range of kits started with a GWR tubular steel post bracket type which went out of production some years ago. I have long been pressing Roger Webster to give us a new version of it and I understand that development is now underway. As noted below, the range of kits in this category was expanded during the late 1960s and '70s.

There was a further change in 1978 when four different varieties of GWR straight post (the square timber type) signal were introduced in fully assembled form, with glazed spectacle plates and pre-coloured arms. These are now sold in ready-to-assemble form but still have pre-coloured arms and glazed spectacle plates. They were supplemented in 1982 by a similar kit for a GWR bracket two doll splitting signal, and then, a year later, by similar kits for LMS pattern (straight post) stop and distant signals. In 1984, SR stop and distant signals with railbuilt posts were added to the range. These used a whitemetal casting for the railbuilt post. They were joined by a combined stop and

lower arm distant during 1985.

All these kits are in 4mm scale, although GWR straight post pattern stop and distant signal kits have since been produced in 7mm scale.

The result of these developments is that the present range of 4mm scale model signals comprises three distinct categories:

1 Full kit form with all the individual components on sprues.

2 Ready-to-assemble signals incorporating glazed spectacle plates and pre-coloured arms.

3 The SR railbuilt pattern signal with cast whitemetal post.

Of these three types, the first currently includes kits

Ratio's cast whitemetal post is a great aid to modelling railbuilt signals such as this one, photographed at Adlestone during 1993. Photo: Mike Romans

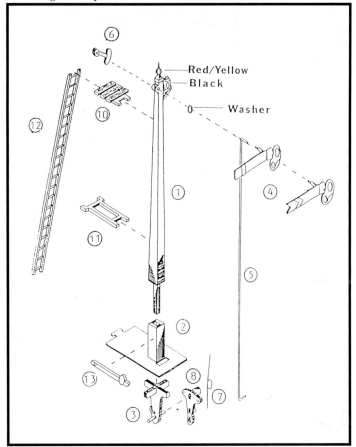

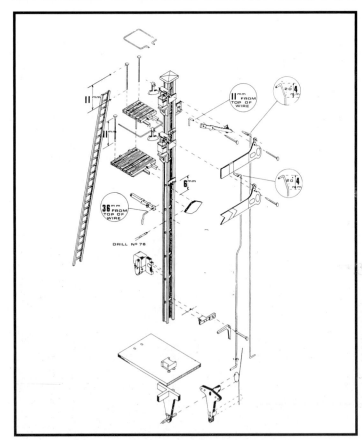

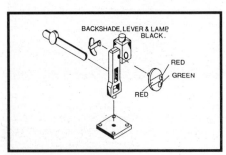

Top: A small bracket from a standard tubular post - you can reproduce this signal from Ratio kit [476].
Bottom: An LMS Pratt truss gantry at Llandudno. Photos: Mike Romans

the most readily achievable.

The LMS kit is reasonably well suited to later LNER, or Eastern Region and Scottish Region usage, albeit with a few minor detail discrepancies. The SR railbuilt type signal is, of course, unique to the Southern's lines and some parts of the Somerset & Dorset.

The plastic arms, in my view, capture very well the solid appearance of a timber signal arm and are in many ways better than an etching to represent the turned-over rims of enamelled steel arms. You might be tempted to replace the arms with etchings but, unless you require a special that Ratio doesn't provide in the range, I would be inclined not to bother.

Most of these signals are fairly easy to link into Ratio's cord operating system and, with a touch of weathering, are a good way to set about signalling a layout.

The true kits

I refer to these as 'true' kits because what you get is a set of plastic mouldings, some wire and brief, but good, instructions which cover both assembly and some possible uses and siting arrangements. (The wire, incidentally, now comes in straight lengths; it used to be great fun trying to straighten the coil that Ratio once supplied.)

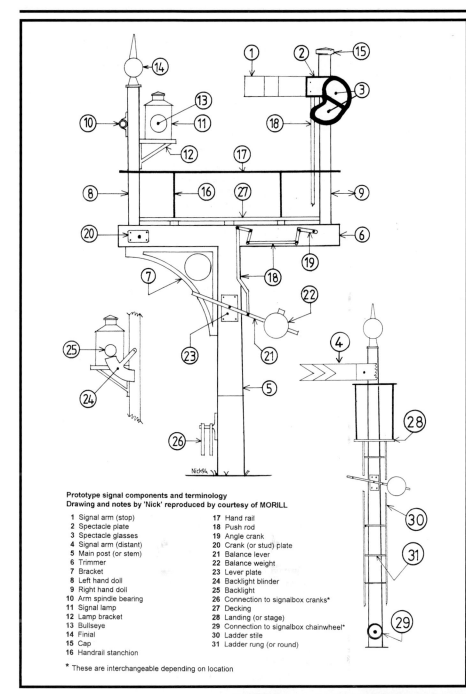

Prototype signal components and terminology
Drawing and notes by 'Nick' reproduced by courtesy of MORILL

1 Signal arm (stop)	17 Hand rail
2 Spectacle plate	18 Push rod
3 Spectacle glasses	19 Angle crank
4 Signal arm (distant)	20 Crank (or stud) plate
5 Main post (or stem)	21 Balance lever
6 Trimmer	22 Balance weight
7 Bracket	23 Lever plate
8 Left hand doll	24 Backlight blinder
9 Right hand doll	25 Backlight
10 Arm spindle bearing	26 Connection to signalbox cranks*
11 Signal lamp	27 Decking
12 Lamp bracket	28 Landing (or stage)
13 Bullseye	29 Connection to signalbox chainwheel*
14 Finial	30 Ladder stile
15 Cap	31 Ladder rung (or round)
16 Handrail stanchion	

* These are interchangeable depending on location

The prototype information in the instructions is limited to sketches, but to a good standard of prototypical accuracy – I wish some other manufacturers could also get that bit right. The instructions are certainly comprehensive enough to cover assembly as intended, and there is little to add to them. However, some very basic modifications and titivation are possible, which I detail below.

Although Ratio's publicity material claims that the kits are only suitable for the 'more experienced modeller', they shouldn't prove too difficult for a determined novice.

In some ways the kits show their age and they certainly require more work than the ready-to-assemble variety. But they are generally fairly accurate renderings of the prototypes and the quality of the mouldings remains good. They are certainly a testimony to the standards of tooling at Ratio – the delicacy of moulding on the finer components remains an example to others. In their early days, these kits did much to bring signals to model railways and they should not be ignored in comparison with the more recent etched offerings in this field.

Ratio's most recent introduction in the signals range is a 4mm scale kit for GWR shunting (ground disc) signals. It includes enough components to make four signals to the cast-base style introduced around 1920 and is intended to produce non-operational models. The kit is a little fiddly, but provides an ideal finishing touch for a well signalled layout. I measured a prototype arm (the one that lives in my garage – haven't you got one?) and the red band scales out at exactly 1mm. You need a fine brush and a steady hand (or some transfer material) to reproduce the band neatly. Incidentally, don't put a yellow band on these signals if they represent GWR (that is, pre-1948) practice.

Apart from being built as Ratio intended, the use of plastic facilitates a lot of simple modifications and crosskitting. The kits are an ideal, relatively inexpen-

A Ratio Pratt truss gantry on Wolverhampton MRC's 4mm scale layout 'Leighford'. Photo: Tony Wright

Ratio signals and signal box on the P4 layout 'Llwynmawr'. The GWR 4-wheel carriage is Ratio kit [613]. Photo: Tony Wright, courtesy of *British Railway Modelling*

sive, introduction to the world of signalling and, with them, there can be little excuse for omitting signalling on a layout portraying almost any British railway company in the post-grouping period. You might not be able to get all the details absolutely right but adaptation of the kits will certainly let you capture the general atmosphere and appearance of signalling on any of the 'Big Four' railways.

Assembly and painting

There is not too much to add to Ratio's instructions, but these few tips may prove useful to readers.

Small components (lamp cases, for example) are best painted while still on the sprue. This is definitely the case with the arms, although you need to partially separate them from the runners before painting. Very carefully separate any area of the arm proper which is joined to the runner but leave it still attached to the sprue. This will allow you to paint it while it is still easy to handle. Alternatively you can completely separate and prepare the arm, and then insert the wire arm spindle *overlength* to provide ease of handling the arm during painting. However, it's not then so easy to store the arm while it dries.

Painting the arms is the key to getting a nice appearance with these kits and I have very fixed views on getting decent results. Prototype signal arms were painted with gloss paint, unless, of course, they were stove enamelled. Gloss paint will weather but on signal arms it is (or should be) subject to regular cleaning. So, in my view, the best appearance comes from using gloss paint on arms representing enamelled prototypes.

The original Humbrol Railway Colours included very accurate renderings of Signal Red and Signal Yellow, but alas these are no longer available. However, there are some quite good colours available to-

day. Don't use 'bufferbeam' red, whatever you do – it's too orange.

Always paint (or spray) a thin coat of gloss white all over the coloured portion of all arms as an undercoat – it will improve the depth of the finishing colour. Once this coat is really hard (rather than just dry), apply the finishing colours in the appropriate areas. This should include a second thin coat of white on the band on the face of the stop arms. Incidentally, the colour of the face of the arm should be continued onto the top and bottom edges.

When all this has hardened, do any touching-up and then paint the spectacle plate in the relevant colour. The advantage of waiting for the paint to harden is that you can usually gently wipe off any paint that you get in the wrong place.

One thing to remember when painting the GWR signals is that the colour of the ball of the finial matched that of the arm. For a stop signal, the finial ball should be red and for a distant signal yellow. Some signals carried stop and distant arms on the same post; the stop arm was always at the top and this configuration was termed a 'stop signal with lower arm distant' The finial ball was painted red on this type of signal.

Another nice touch is to glaze the spectacle plates – and nowadays that is far easier than it might sound. First, you have to carefully drill out and clean up the holes in the spectacle plates, using a small drill in a pin vice. This is not too difficult, except perhaps on the GWR timber arms; these have very narrow rims around the spectacles. Filling the holes is the easiest part of this task, thanks to a technique borrowed from non-railway areas of modelling. This is liquid glazing.

You can use the original American product which is brand-named Crystal Clear, Humbrol's Clear Fix or Carr's Window

Glaze. Colour the resulting clear glazed film with either felt pens (by Tamiya, nice dark colours) or a translucent colour from Tamiya in their transparent acrylic range. To find these products, try the suppliers listed in Appendix 1 or find a model shop covering the aeronautical and military fields. Unfortunately, not all specialist model railway shops stock them.

Generally, do the rest following Ratio's instructions; they built the kits before they wrote them, so they represent a sensible approach.

Kitbashing

Kitbashing or crosskitting these kits is something which is only limited by your imagination and relevant prototype photographs or drawings. As the previous chapters of this book have shown, plastic is easy to work with simple tools and easy to join with the adhesives detailed elsewhere. To modify the signals, you'll need a razor saw, needle files, a craft knife or scalpel, a few small drill bits, and some fine abrasive paper.

Because many prototype signal components came as stock items you simply use the Ratio components in roughly the same fashion as the original workshops used their standard bits.

You can also take advantage of history and inter-company standardisation to replicate some of the other things done with the prototype components. The results might not be absolutely accurate but, because Ratio have got most of the proportions looking good, your results will look well enough for all but the most fastidious scale fanatic.

The kits provide:
LNWR kit [477] Wooden dolls suited to early LMS and some LNER use.

LNER kit [486] Corrugated arms and 'visible' lattice posts and dolls suited to early LNER, LMS and SR use.

GWR kit [466] Wooden post and dolls adaptable to other uses with a little cutting and scraping.

GWR kit [467] The later pattern of steel arms can be used to update [466] signals in the same way that the GWR and Western Region did.

LMS kit [476] Tubular steel posts and dolls and some bracket components suited to LNER, Eastern Region and Scottish Region use; post-1930s enamel steel arms suitable for most companies and Regions, except the GWR/WR. Because the components are reasonably dimensionally accurate, it's easy to model a signal from a photograph without the need for a drawing. For instance, all the bracket signal main uprights automatically place the bracket landing at a correct height and straight post signal heights are readily adjusted downwards by cutting. Raising the height of straight post signals is simplest with the tubular steel types because the prototype posts didn't have the taper of a timber post.

You can also use a combination of bits to copy prototypical changes that were made to signals already in place. An example is adding London Midland Region upper quadrant arms to Western Region tubular steel posts (but keep the finials) as happened when the LMR took over some former GWR routes. More obviously, you can use the arms and some other bits from either the LMS or LNER kit to modernise the LNWR signals to upper quadrant.

We'll look at a few examples in a moment, but first the Pratt truss gantry. This is pure LMS and is completely wrong if you are modelling a gantry on any other company's lines. It does, however, have another use. With minor changes it is very close to the style of gantry used for colour light signals by the LMR on non-electrified lines and on the WR in the 1960s and '70s. The Scottish Region also used this style on at least one scheme. Add some suitably detailed Eckon/CCH signal heads and you're away.

Ratio semaphore signal kitbashing I have done in the past has produced several interesting signals. An early LMS upper quadrant stop signal featured a short timber post made from a doll out of the LNWR kit, with arm and fittings from the LMS kit. A modernised LMS lattice bracket used the main bracket upright from the LNER kit and the landing and doll from the LMS kit. Either of these could have used the corrugated arms from the LNER kit.

Another nice little mixture resulted from using the lattice main upright, bracket and landing from the LNER kit, a timber doll from the LNWR kit, and arms from the LMS kit to produce an LNER variant.

LNER timber post signals can be produced with a bit of judicious fettling of either the LNWR or GWR square posts, although some of the LNWR ones have the distinctive 'bulge' that was, I think, unique to that company.

The full range of what you can produce by mixing components from various kits is best established from study of prototype photos and a spot of imagination. Fortunately, the modular nature of the kits automatically creates reasonably accurate proportions, so don't worry too much about the scale drawings.

Mechanical reliability and operation
Over the years, various magazine articles have suggested using etched components to replace the plastic fittings supplied in the kits. The main areas recommended for this treatment are the arms (which I've already discussed) and such things

as the cranks and linkages. There is no doubt that, in the interests of strength, the Ratio components in the latter area are a bit overscale, particularly thickness (which for most such components would scale to just under 5thou in 4mm scale). But, that said, these components aren't too obtrusive, and if properly assembled they are plenty strong enough to do the job. For several years I had a GWR stop signal worked by a cord with a run of 5ft. To return the signal to danger, there was a hefty coil spring which put a lot of tension on the mechanical bits. They survived without any problem, despite the wild temperature variations of a loft.

The key to getting this area right is not necessarily to change the components but to correctly assemble those supplied. All the moving components need to be a good sliding or rotating fit. The instructions recommend using appropriate size twist drills for this job and you should definitely do a lot of fitting and trying as you go. Do not allow any slop to develop as you clear holes; this will be fatal, especially in the arm pivots.

As a guide, the fit to aim for is such that an upper quadrant arm will readily fall to danger under its own weight before it is connected, via the operating rod, to the cranks and so on. With this degree of free movement, you can dispense with Ratio's wire for the operating rod (but still use it for arm and crank pivots) and replace it with fine florists' wire which you can get in straight lengths.

Paint, or chemically blacken, florists' wire; it's made of iron and will rust easily. Even the plated stuff will rust, especially around the cut ends where the plating finishes. Although I haven't tried it, I don't see why you couldn't use fine fishing line to connect the balance weight to the arm on straight post upper quadrant signals. Mind you, the knots will be fun.

Ratio signals are quite suitable for the well known 'wire in tube' type of operation and are also easy to adapt to operation by means of thread or fishing line. You can also, of course, use Ratio's own operating system. Conversion to electric activation requires use of a relay with a gainstroke extended arm, or homemade solenoid coils sited below the baseboard.

Ratio signal kits and components

2mm scale
260 Lower quadrant (stop and distant arms provided)
262 Lower quadrant bracket (stop and distant arms provided)
263 Ground signals (four)
270 Upper quadrant (stop and distant arms provided)
271 Pratt truss gantry

4mm scale ready-to-assemble
460 GWR square post stop signal
461 GWR square post distant signal
462 GWR square post stop signal with lower arm distant
469 GWR square post bracket sig-

nal (provided with two stop arms and two distant arms)
470 LMS tubular post stop signal
471 LMS tubular post distant signal

4mm scale SR railbuilt post signal kits (some whitemetal components)
490 SR railbuilt post stop signal
491 SR railbuilt post distant signal
492 SR railbuilt post stop signal with lower arm distant

4mm scale signal kits
465 Ground signals (four)
466 GWR square post signals (components for up to four signals, including brackets)
467 GWR tubular post signals (components for two signals)
476 LMS tubular post signals (components for up to four signals, including brackets)
477 LNWR square post signals (components for up to four signals, including brackets)
486 LNER lattice post signals (components for up to four signals, including brackets; corrugated arms; can be converted to SR lattice types)
478 Pratt truss gantry

7mm scale signal kits
071 GWR square post signal (stop and distant arms provided)

Signal components
250 2mm scale cord control system
134 Signal levers (pair)
135 4mm scale cord control system
136 Cord control extension pack
137 Signal arms with lenses, long and short types

Note: for prices (as of January 1996), see Appendix 5.

The prototype is still there to be studied. Photographs like this one, taken in early 1996, are an aid to getting the details right. Photo: Leon C Kidd

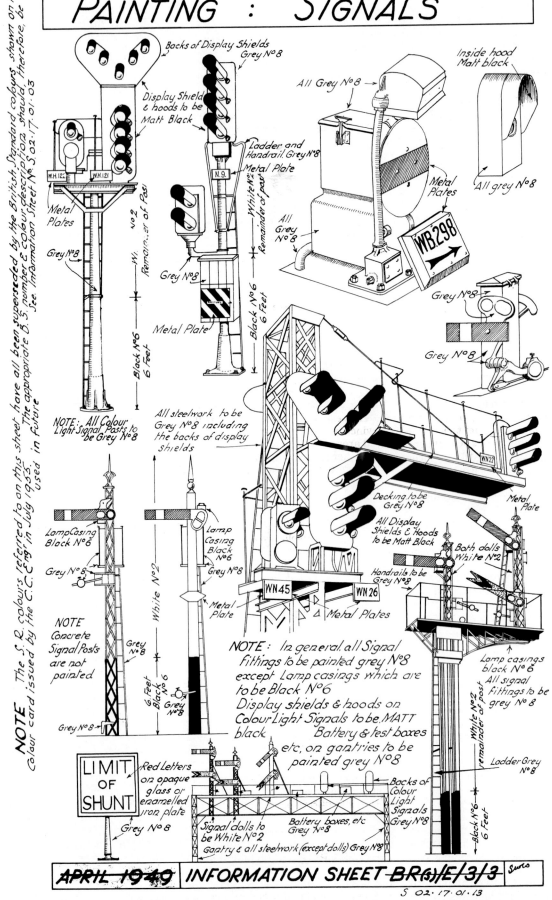

BRITISH RAILWAYS : SOUTHERN REGION
CHIEF CIVIL ENGINEER'S DEPARTMENT
PAINTING : SIGNALS

NOTE. The S.R. colours referred to on this sheet have all been superseded by the British Standard colours shown on the Colour card issued by the C.C.Eng in July 1955. The appropriate B.S. number & colour description should, therefore, be used in future. See Information Sheet No S.02.17.01.03

Backs of Display Shields Grey Nº 8

Display Shield & hoods to be Matt Black

Ladder and Handrail. Grey Nº 8

White Nº2

Metal Plate

Inside hood Matt black

All Grey Nº 8

Metal Plates

All grey Nº 8

Metal Plates

Grey Nº 8

W.H.122. W.H.121.

No 2 Remainder of Post

All Grey Nº 8

WB.298

Grey Nº 8

Grey Nº 8

Metal Plate

Black Nº 6 6 Feet

White Nº2 Remainder of post

Grey Nº 8

N. 9.

Black Nº6 6 Feet

NOTE: All Colour Light Signal Posts to be Grey Nº 8

All steelwork to be Grey Nº 8 including the backs of display shields

Lamp Casing Black Nº 6

Grey Nº 8

Lamp Casing Black Nº 6

Grey Nº 8

White Nº 2

Metal Plate

WN 22

Decking to be Grey Nº 8

Metal Plate

All Display Shields & Hoods to be Matt Black

Both dolls White Nº 2

Handrails to be Grey Nº 8

NOTE Concrete Signal Posts are not painted

Grey Nº 8

WN 45

WN 26

Metal Plates

Grey Nº 8

6 Feet Black Nº 6

Grey Nº 8

Grey Nº 8

Lamp casings black Nº 6

All signal fittings to be grey Nº 8

NOTE: In general all Signal fittings to be painted grey Nº8 except Lamp casings which are to be Black Nº6 Display shields & hoods on Colour Light Signals to be MATT black Battery & test boxes etc, on gantries to be painted grey Nº8

LIMIT OF SHUNT

Red Letters on opaque glass or enamelled iron plate

Grey Nº 8

Signal dolls to be White Nº 2

Gantry & all steelwork (except dolls) Grey Nº 8

Battery boxes, etc Grey Nº 8

Backs of Colour Light Signals Grey Nº 8

Ladder Grey Nº 8

White Nº 2 remainder of post

Black Nº 6 6 Feet

APRIL 1949   INFORMATION SHEET BR(s)E/3/3

S 02.17.01.13

Chapter Eight
PAINTING

A study for painting. Notice how light and prominent the mortar courses are and how the darker and lighter bricks stand out. There's been a noticeable attempt to seal the ridge tiles to the right of the chimney. Look at the range of tones on the door (best reproduced on the model by dry brushing) and the peeling paint on the window frames. As you can see, the real world looks matt - nothing in this picture, not even the window glass, has a hint of glossiness. Photo: N I Binns

Although this is the last chapter, the process it deals with – painting, finishing, weathering and surface treatment – should not be seen as a single one-off operation to be left until construction is complete. Rather, it is an integral part of that construction, something to be planned into the assembly order from the outset. Many of the components are best painted before they are installed on the model or, quite often, before they are even removed from the sprue.

There are very few books on painting models. One of the best, at least for rolling stock and locomotives, is *Painting and Lining in the Smaller Scales* by master painter Steve Barnfield, a sister volume to this handbook.

I haven't attempted to give details of railway companies' painting schemes - there were far too many - but I have included a couple of specimen paint specification sheets as examples.

Approach
In Chapter 2, I have already outlined a few of the considerations that shape my approach to painting a model. Chief among them is consistency – will the finished article blend in with the other models around it and into the overall scene?

I have also mentioned the strength of colour and the use of unifying tone to blend each individual element into the whole. To reproduce the softening effect that atmospheric dust and pollution have on colours seen from a distance, a little white (and, in some cases, a touch of blue) added to colours will produce a realistic effect. This is especially true for models that will be at the back of a layout.

On the whole, you should avoid strong 'pure' colours, especially black and white. These need toning down if they are not to leap out and shout 'model' at the viewer. A tiny amount of browny-black will reduce the starkness of 'out of the tin' white to a more natural looking very pale grey. At the other end of the scale, a little red or brown will warm up and soften black. Often a very dark grey will look far more convincing than 'real' black, even in shadowed areas.

Another rule (insofar as there are any hard and fast rules for painting) is to avoid gloss finishes. Matt will almost always look unobtrusively natural but gloss will stick out like a sore thumb.

That said, if everything is painted in a uniformly flat finish, the effect will be an equally unnatural deadening. There is a wide gradation of finishes between high gloss and absolute matt. The halfway mark is usually referred to as a sheen finish.

The degree of flatness or glossiness of a paint can be varied easily. For example, matt varnish can be added to gloss finishes, gloss varnish to flat ones and, of course, matt and gloss paints can be mixed together.

You can exploit this range of finishes in your model painting. To take just one example, the body of an open coal wagon will be matt (and the inside should even have a slightly gritty finish) but areas like the axleboxes, brake linkages and buffer heads can have a dull sheen. Carriages (and road vehicles for that matter) can have a higher sheen, but avoid too glossy a finish.

About the only place where a really gloss finish is valid is modelled water – open water tanks, ponds, rivers and, of course, puddles. Varnish is the usual way of representing these.

The colour photographs in this book show some examples of how a kitbuilt model can be enhanced by careful, thoughtful painting. By studying the photographs, you may pick up some ideas you can use yourself. But, as always, beware of simply cloning; as I've said before, making a model of a model will rarely result in realism. Let the prototype be your final arbiter.

Paints
There are many ranges and types of modelling paint, some more easily obtained than others. By far the most popular among railway modellers is Humbrol enamel. It comes in two sizes of tin (or 'tinlet') and can be found in most toy, craft, and hobby shops. Most of the models illustrated in this book were painted with Humbrol. There is an extensive range of colours in both matt and gloss, as well as complementary sundries like thinners and varnish.

The principal alternative to enamel is acrylic paint. Humbrol produces a wide range of colours in this medium. Humbrol Acrylic and other brands, notably Tamiya, are sold in many model shops.

Whichever brand or type of paint you choose, it will need stirring thoroughly before use. This is crucial. Failure to stir the paint is one of the commonest causes of disappointment for novice painters.

After a tin has sat on the shelf of the local model shop for a few weeks, all the pigment (the finely ground solids that give the paint its colour and body) will have sunk to the bottom leaving the oils and solvents at the top. It's a good idea to pour about half the liquid into a little cup, stir the tin until the pigment is fully mixed with the remainder, then return the decanted portion and thoroughly stir it in.

It takes several minutes to stir a new tin of modelling enamel properly, a process that needs repeating each time it is used after standing for more than a couple of days. Don't be tempted to cut corners here – *it's vital to stir the paint thoroughly*.

Once you've finished with the tin, press the lid on firmly. Don't leave tins standing open for long periods. The paint will get progressively thicker and eventually form a skin. Mind you, it'll dry out eventually whatever you do. Don't bother trying to reconstitute old, heavily skinned or dried out paint. Throw it away and buy a new tin.

Both enamel and acrylic modellers' paints take well to styrene, so there is seldom any need for a separate primer on plastic models. But neither type of paint will take well on bare metal, especially brass. So if you are building a Ratio kit that includes etched components or have added various metal bits and pieces of your own devising, you will need to prime them. The quickest (and probably the cheapest) way is to buy a small can of aerosol primer from your local auto factors or branch of Halfords.

BRITISH RAILWAYS : SOUTHERN REGION
CHIEF CIVIL ENGINEER'S DEPARTMENT
PAINTING : GATES

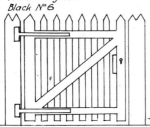

To be painted similar colour to adjacent fencing, usually Stone Nº1 Metal Hinges, Lock, etc. to be Black Nº6

WICKET GATE

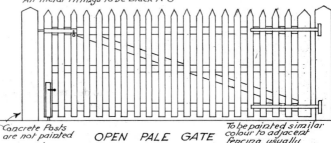

All metal fittings to be Black Nº6

Concrete Posts are not painted

OPEN PALE GATE

To be painted similar colour to adjacent fencing, usually Stone Nº1A

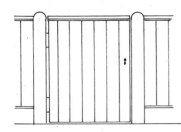

CLOSE BOARDED GATE

To be painted similar colours to adjacent fencing: Stone Nº1A with Green Nº 3A Capping

Concrete Posts are not painted

METAL GATES

All Green Nº3A If not previously tarred or galvanized

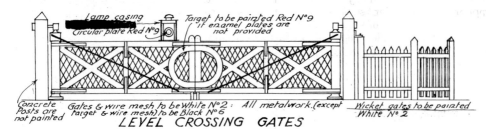

Lamp casing
Circular plate Red Nº9
Target to be painted Red Nº9 if enamel plates are not provided

Concrete Posts are not painted

Gates & wire mesh to be White Nº2 : All metalwork.(except target & wire mesh) to be Black Nº6

Wicket gates to be painted White Nº2

LEVEL CROSSING GATES

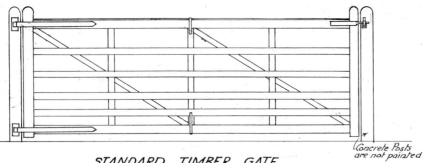

Concrete Posts are not painted

STANDARD TIMBER GATE

All Stone Nº1 : Metal Fittings Black Nº6
Where these gates are used at certain Crossings, etc, it is left to the discretion of the Divisional Engineer as to whether White Nº2 should be used in place of Stone Nº1

NOTE
The S.R colours referred to on this sheet have all been superseded by the British Standard colours shown on the colour card issued by the C.C.Eng on July 1955. The appropriate B.S.number & colour description should therefore be used in future. See Information Sheet Nº S.02.17.01.03

| SEP.T 1949 | INFORMATION SHEET B.P.et E/5/1 | SW.D |

S. 02. 17. 01. 15

You will probably find a choice of acrylic or cellulose primer in white, grey or red oxide (a sort of browny-red). Colour is up to you and depends on what colour you will be putting over the primer. Grey, being neutral, is the safest choice. As to the paint itself, acrylic primer smells less unpleasant than cellulose and is far less likely to damage moulded styrene. On the other hand, I think the cellulose offers better adhesion.

Again, thoroughly mixing the paint is vital. Shake the can vigorously until you hear the little metal agitator rattling around in the can. Then keep shaking. Two or three minutes is the absolute minimum. Keep shaking at intervals while you are using the can.

Other materials you may need include both gloss and matt varnish. It's far cheaper to buy gloss varnish in 'proper' sized tins from a DIY superstore rather than pay through the nose for a modelling tinlet. Not that you'll be using much. On the other hand, you'll get through plenty of matt varnish. It can be used to give an overall unifying and protective coat to completed models, so it is better to buy it in aerosol form. Most modellers' ranges include spray cans of matt varnish. An alternative is artists' fixative which you can buy from any art shop or graphics suppliers. It's not cheap, though.

One of the most under-rated but effective finishing techniques is the use of various 'dry' colours such as crushed chalk, crushed charcoal, or ground artists' pastels. You can also buy dry weathering powders and these can give superb effects.

Many of these paints materials can be obtained from the general suppliers listed in Appendix 1.

Brushes

I will restrict my remarks to ordinary paint brushes. If you've got an airbrush, you probably know more about using it than I do. And if you haven't got one, I'm not about to tell you to buy one. You can paint any Ratio kit perfectly satisfactorily by hand.

The first brush is not for putting paint on. It's for blowing dust off. Camera shops sell 'puffer' brushes, soft bristled and topped with a rubber bulb like an old fashioned car horn. If you can't run to such luxury, use a small good quality soft household paintbrush to dust off models before painting.

For painting, buy the best quality brushes you can afford. If you look after them, they'll last for ages. I always use sable brushes. If you can get hold of them, signwriters' chisels are the ones to go for. The bristles are very good quality, long and springy and they lay flat which makes this type of brush ideal for large areas like carriage sides. A size 3 or 4 should cover most eventualities. Failing that, a Rowney or Windsor & Newton round artists' sable, again size 3 or 4, will do.

For fine work, you need a pointed sable artists' brush. If you can only afford one, get a size 0. But two, a size 1 and a size 00, will give you more scope.

These sables should be used for best, kept scrupulously clean and stored some-

where dry with the bristles well protected. For rougher work, such as painting wagon underframes or getting into nooks and crannies, use a cheaper synthetic artists' brush. There are plenty of brands to choose from.

For dry brush techniques, choose a synthetic with a broad chisel shape and short, springy bristles.

Some of the suppliers listed in Appendix 1 sell brushes by mail order and most craft, hobby and model shops carry a limited stock. But in my view, there's no substitute for a browse round your local art shop. You can see the various shapes and sizes for yourself, compare prices and probably come away having bought far more than you intended.

Techniques

Painting is one of those things that's far easier to do than to describe and the following advice is no substitute for plenty of practice.

With plastic kits, there is not much preparation needed before the model is ready to receive paint. The most important thing is to make sure the surfaces are free of any dust or grease. It's surprising how greasy human skin is and fingerprints, invisible on the bare plastic, will often show through the paint. If it's practical, wash the model gently in lukewarm water with a touch of detergent, rinse thoroughly and leave it overnight to dry. Alternatively, you'll probably get away with a wipe over with white spirit or similar paint thinner. If there are any metal components, they may need priming.

When you are ready to start painting, decant some paint from the tin onto a palette of some sort unless you only need a single brushload of a particular colour. In my case, the palette is often the surface of the bench. But an offcut of styrene sheet, a coffee jar lid or something equally informal is better.

Using a palette, rather than working straight from the tin, means that the colours don't get contaminated by each other. It also stops the paint in the tin drying up and helps keep dust and general workshop grot out of it.

You can mix up the exact colour you require on your palette and, by using the appropriate thinner, adjust the consistency of the paint so that it flows as you want it to. For dry brushing, the paint should be as thick as possible, for general painting about as runny as double cream and for overall washes fairly wet. Experiment.

For plain painting, load the brush fairly generously, keep the paint thinned down enough to flow freely without flooding, and work reasonably quickly. Spread the paint evenly over the surface with a series of firm criss-cross strokes. Once the brush is fairly empty, go back over the area with long, light strokes in one direction only, to smooth the paint and lose any brush marks. This is known as laying off.

If you have a large surface to cover, it's easier to paint it as a series of smaller areas. Make sure you have enough paint mixed to cover the whole surface and work

quickly so that you don't get a discernible fuzzy border where each area overlaps its neighbour. This occurs as wet paint is brushed over the previous coat just as it has started to dry. The mark, called a dry edge, can be eased out by picking up a little – a *very* little – thinner on the brush and merging it in.

Dry brushing is an entirely different matter. Here the idea is to keep the paint

Use a brush with short stiff-ish bristles to dry brush moulded relief.

and brush as dry as possible, use the lightest touch and deposit as little paint as you can. It is specifically a technique for highlighting raised relief, rather than covering an area.

The paint needs to be as thick as you can get it. If some of the pigment has settled at the bottom of the tin, scoop a little out with a match stick. It will be nice and pastey. Otherwise, decant a little paint on to a scrap of plastic or an old tin lid and leave it while you do something else. The solvent will start to evaporate and the paint will thicken up a treat.

Dry brushing calls for a stiffish springy brush. Don't use your best ones. Load a little of the thick paint onto the tip then work the brush lightly on a sheet of tissue paper to remove the excess. Work the brush over the surface with a light touch, barely kissing the work with the tip of the bristles.

Weathering

As painting is to assembly, so weathering is to painting. It must be an integral part of the finishing process, not an afterthought tagged on to the end.

The colours and tones of the model, how matt it is, the texture of both the paintwork and the underlying surface, the amount of distressing and so on are all part of the weathering process.

Weathering is very easy to do badly. Simply smearing a little grey or brown paint around the base of a building or washing a hitherto pristine wagon with 'dirtied' paint thinner is not weathering.

Three of the most effective techniques for additional weathering on a model (additional in the sense that much of the weathering will have been done during the preparation and painting stages) are dry brushing, streaking and applying dry colour.

Dry brushing is described above. You can use the technique to represent several prototype effects. For instance, dirt is washed onto the bottom of a wall dur-

Ratio kits suit modern image layouts; this ex-Midland Rly signal box was photgraphed at Kirkby In Ashfield a couple of years ago. Its paintwork looks in pretty good order. In recent years, with the sectorisation and privatisation of the railways, standardised colour schemes seem a thing of the past. Magazines like *RAIL* will help you keep up with the colour changes and, of course, you can do a little field research. Photo: Mike Romans

they did twenty or a hundred years ago. The effects of weather are timeless. Wood bleaches and splits, paint fades and peels, steel and iron rust, window panes get coated in grime or crack. All these effects – the essential details that add a patina of age, use and authenticity to a model – are there for you to observe, record and reproduce in miniature.

Two of the main influences on how a particular model should be weathered are the influence of climate, especially sunlight and humidity, and the effects of pollution.

Climatic effects, the action of 'real' weather, will depend on the geographical location of your structures. Paint will fade much more rapidly in the strong sunlight of the south-east than in the cloudier north west. Consider whether your line runs

Concrete posts often develop a rough, speckled appearance as you can observe on the prototype fence and gradient posts. This effect has been reproduced on the Ratio model by 'misting' the post with a dark grey car aerosol.

ing rain, is splashed there by traffic or is carried up as dust in dry weather. There will be a gentle gradation in the discoloration of the wall. The lower you get, the dirtier. Careful dry brushing, working up from the bottom, will avoid a distinct edge where one tone merges into another. Similarly, mould growth is seldom sharply defined. Nor is it a dense green, obscuring the wall behind. Dry brushing a mix of grey-green is the best way to ensure a seamless patch through which the underlying wall colour can be seen.

Streaking, on the other hand, is a wet technique. It can be used to represent lime scale and stain, rain streaks, rust from joints in gutters and downpipes or streaks of dirt from under window cills. Here again the key is moderation. Having decided the appropriate colour, dilute it with thinners until it is fairly runny. Use as little paint as possible. Begin by placing a few spots at the point where the stain or streak is to start. Wipe the surplus from the brush and draw the spots downwards. When they have just begun to dry, moisten the brush with thinner and work down the streaks, spreading and diluting them as

you go. After another drying period, repeat the process with the brush a bit wetter, this time concentrating on the edges of the streak. You can see the effect in one of the colour photographs.

Dry colours will give you a whole arsenal of subtle weathering weapons. As well as the commercially produced weathering powders and crushed chalk, charcoal and pastels mentioned above, you can also use powder paints. Obviously avoid bright colours. The powders can be gently 'washed' on with a soft brush, stippled on with a stiffer one, smeared on with tissue or dabbed on with a duster. They can also be blown, sprinkled or dusted onto wet paint to give surface texture and tone down colour.

There are far more weathering techniques than I have space to describe but, as with so many aspects of modelling, the 'how' is much less important than the 'why'. Whatever techniques you adopt, you will only get convincing, realistic results if you have thought about the effect you are trying to reproduce. And that, once again, means going back to the prototype.

Even if you model the 1930s or earlier, personal observation is all-important when it comes to weathering. The steam age railway may be long gone but brickwork still suffers frost damage as it always has. Moss, lichens and greenery creep up walls in 1996 just as they did in 1923 or whenever. Disfiguring rain streaks on buildings today look much as

from east to west or from north to south and which point of the compass each building faces. Colours will be more faded on the south aspect and there will be more algae or lichen growth on north facing walls. Is a building in shadow or under trees? If so, moss may flourish. From which side does the prevailing wind blow, carrying with it the smoke and soot from chimneys or industry? Winds are predominantly from the south-west in much of England, but less so as you go north and east.

The main effect of pollution (at least, as regards weathering) is that by depositing solid matter, it can darken (or, in the case of cement works and some quarries, lighten) and discolour surfaces. The nature of the pollution (and hence its visible effects) will depend on many factors, so you will need to think about the geographical, industrial and historical setting of your layout.

Painting architectural surfaces

In the following notes, I have concentrated on Ratio's buildings, structures and other lineside models. Mike Romans has looked at painting signals in Chapter 7 and rolling stock is covered in *Painting and Lining in the Smaller Scales*. There's also a chapter devoted to painting goods stock in *Getting the Best from Plastic Wagon Kits*, another title in this series. Details of both books can be found in Appendix 1.

Unpainted wood. Fences, barn doors, telegraph poles, pallets, timber huts and so on vary enormously in colour. They are seldom nut brown, although that is the colour they are most often painted on model railways. Newly creosoted wood will be almost black and freshly sawn timber a sandy colour but both will gradually fade to a very light grey. Try to vary the colour subtly and paint with, rather than across, the 'grain'.

Brickwork. Providing the model is moulded in an appropriate colour of styrene (usually a light browny red or, in certain circumstances a bluey slate grey), you can get away with the lazy man's method. Mix up a fairly thin mortar colour. A creamy grey will be fine for most mortar but look out for local variations. Wash this over the surface of the brickwork, making sure it settles into the moulded recesses of the mortar courses. Leave it to dry for a few minutes then, using a pad of tissue or cloth, wipe it from the surface of the bricks. Work diagonally so that you are not wiping along either vertical or horizontal courses. Any residual paint on the faces of the bricks will help weaken the contrast and tone the overall colour down.

For a more satisfying and realistic effect, run mortar colour into the courses and clean it from the face of the bricks as above then leave it to dry thoroughly. Mix up a colour fairly close to that of the plastic brickwork. This will be used to pick out individual bricks. By adding a drop of darker or lighter colour to each brushload, you can vary the basic mix almost brick by brick. Paint the bricks carefully with a size 1 or size 0 pointed sable brush. To get a reasonable effect, you need to do about a third of the total, evenly spread. The final stage is to unify the painted and unpainted bricks by dry brushing the whole surface with a slightly lighter version of the basic brick colour. Take care not to let the dry brushed paint obliterate the mortar courses.

Stone walls. The technique is very similar to that for brick. Depending on what stone you wish to portray, you can opt for a little more variety of colour than with brickwork. Sandstone can be any colour from tawny yellow to rusty red, granite varies from a muddy pink to a bluey grey and limestone ranges from dark grey to a warmish cream. Virtually every stone can be a slightly different shade, if you can be bothered to paint them all individually. Adding fairly coarse dry colour will give the stones some surface texture. Mortar courses may be anything from dark grey to a light cream, depending on location and age.

Roofs. Slates and tiles are treated much the same as brickwork. The colours used will depend on what material is being represented. Beware of Humbrol's Slate Grey; it's too dark for slates that have been on a roof for years. You can usually get a convincing effect by painting the whole roof in the appropriate basic colour, leaving it to dry, picking out a few individual slates or tiles in a slightly lighter or darker shade then lightly dry brushing a unifying coat overall. You don't need to pick out as many as with brickwork nor make them contrast as strongly. Finally, a very little darker grey (for tiles) or reddy brown (for tiles) dry brushed upwards will give the overlap of the courses a bit of emphasis.

Corrugated iron. When new, this material is galvanised, making it a silvery colour. It very soon fades to a dull, flat light grey. Real corrugated iron roofs are often painted, however. Red oxide and dark green are the favoured colours around my part of the Midlands but I'm sure it varies from area to area. You can draw in the joints between the sheets (they are usually 3ft wide or 12mm in 4mm scale) with a very fine pen if you wish. Corrugated iron roofs soon start to rust, varying from quite an orangey colour for new rust to a dark reddy brown for older corrosion. The first places where rust will show are along the lower edges of the sheets and around the nail holes.

Painted woodwork. The finish can be anything from dead matt for well weathered paint to a medium sheen for newly decorated areas. The older the paintwork, the more washed out and faded the colour should be. Railway structures, fences, station woodwork, signal boxes and so on tended to be kept fairly well painted. The actual colours used were set out on painting sheets so a little research is called for. Generally, Ratio's instructions include reliable guides to railway company colours.

Concrete. Although you wouldn't think so to judge by most model railways, concrete is seldom grey, at least not the cold grey you get by mixing black and white. The colour of new concrete depends to a large extent on the aggregate it is made from. It usually ranges from a whitish beige to a warm tawny grey. Humbrol's Concrete Colour is a good starting point and it can be doctored with white, mid grey and dark earth. I sometimes add a drop of tan or beige to warm things up a bit.

Location and use affect the colour. Near industrial sites and beside mainline railways, concrete structures will become dirty, soot-stained and dark. In the country, beside minor railways, they will be much lighter. In damp, shaded sheltered conditions, concrete soon becomes colonised by moss, lichens and other surface plants. On the other hand, if it is exposed to strong sunlight, it will become bleached.

Newly cast concrete is smooth but well weathered old concrete develops a very gritty, pebbly texture. To represent this, paint the basic colour on and let it dry. Then, using a stiff brush, stipple on a few spots of dry-ish light cream. When this is dry, do the same with a darker colour. Another way of 'speckling' the concrete (particularly posts) is to make a quick, light pass over the model with a matt dark grey car aerosol. I used this trick on the concrete lamp posts illustrated in this book.

Concrete is seldom used alone structurally, except to form foundations. It is almost always reinforced by a steel mesh embedded within it. Posts, facings and panels, piles and stanchions, platforms, huts, bridges and other structures all rely on steel reinforcement.

Concrete is slightly porous and, in older structures, it develops cracks. Water gets in and corrodes the embedded steel. Very frequently the rust will stain the surface of the concrete, particularly in corners and at the ends of beams, lintels, and panels. On vertical surfaces, rust stains will be washed down walls and posts by the rain, leaving lighter and browner streaks.

Mix the same rust colours as for corrugated iron. Use a small sable brush to paint spots where rust is just breaking through. The streaking technique described earlier can be used to reproduce rust stains on vertical walls. For larger areas of rust discoloration, dry brushing paint or using dry colour will give the best results.

An appropriate picture to finish with. This Ratio GWR brake van [569] was entirely brush painted and weathered in the confines of a tiny narrowboat cabin more years ago than I care to remember. Since then, I've had nearly a quarter of a century's pleasure from Ratio products. I hope that you get great enjoyment and satisfaction out of the range too and I wish you every success with your modelling.

APPENDIX 1
FURTHER INFORMATION AND SOURCES

RATIO PLASTIC MODELS LTD
Ratio plastic kits are sold by many general model and hobby shops and by most model railway specialist retailers. You can also buy them from mail order specialists; some are listed below. Ratio also supply direct to the customer, either by post or to personal callers at their factory showroom.
If you have any problems in obtaining Ratio products or hit any snags assembling them, Ratio will be pleased to advise you.

Ratio Plastic Models Ltd
Hamlyn House
Mardle Way
Buckfastleigh
Devon TQ11 0NS
Telephone: 01364 642764

EXHIBITIONS
I recommend that you attend as many model railway exhibitions as you can. These are listed in most model railway magazines, including the Diary sections of *Modelling Railways Illustrated, Railway Modeller* and *British Railway Modelling*.
At exhibitions, you will see many examples of Ratio models in layout applications. These will give you plenty of inspiration and ideas. You will see various constructional and painting/finishing techniques and will have the opportunity to discuss these with the layout builders and operators. Exhibitions are also a good place to pick up reference material such as books, magazines and photographs, often very cheaply.
There are very few permanent exhibitions. Probably the most famous is Pendon Museum. All Pendon's architectural models are scratchbuilt (mainly from card) so there may seem little obvious connection with plastic kit building at first sight. But the standard of modelling is so high, the scope of the project so breath-taking and the integration of individual models into a cohesive whole so peerless, that any railway modeller visiting Pendon cannot fail to be inspired.

Pendon Museum
Long Wittenham, Abingdon, Oxfordshire, OX14 4QD
Telephone: 01865 407365

Another permanent exhibition worth visiting is Pecorama. Based at the home of Peco products and *Railway Modeller* magazine, Pecorama is more than just an exhibition of model railways. It provides a day out for the whole family with pleasure gardens, a miniature passenger-carrying railway exhibition, refreshments, a model shop and plenty of other activities for children and adults.
The Pecorama display includes over a dozen layouts in several scales, ranging in size from a tiny layout of 1ft 6ins x 4ft 6ins to 21ft x 6ft, as well as the 'Control-a-Train' O gauge outdoor layout which is 37ft x 22ft. Ratio Plastic Models feature on many of the layouts. For details of Pecorama's opening hours and admission prices, write or telephone.

Pecorama
Beer
Seaton
Devon
EX12 3NA - *Telephone:* 01297 21542

MODEL RAILWAY CLUBS
If you are a newcomer to the hobby, it is worth joining your local model railway club. You will find a wealth of experience and expertise among the members, and most of them will be very happy to share it with you.
Some model railway clubs loan tools and equipment which you may wish to use but can't afford to buy. Many clubs also have a library of books which members can borrow.
To locate your nearest club, look out for their exhibition (usually an annual event), ask at your local model shop or study the club or diary pages in model railway magazines. Your local public library may also have the addresses of clubs in your area.

SOCIETIES
As well as local clubs, there are also a number of national organisations dedicated to specific scales and gauges. Those below cater for the scales which Ratio produce models for: 2, 4 and 7mm/1ft.
Please remember the courtesy of enclosing a stamped self-addressed envelope when contacting any of the clubs or societies listed below. Please also mention that you read about them in this *Modelling Railways Illustrated Handbook*

Two Millimetre Association
8 Kent House Lane
Beckenham
Kent, BR3 1LF

N Gauge Society
Membership Secretary
'Foxstones'
Winstone
Cirencester
Glos
GL7 7JU

EM Gauge Society
200A Prospect Road
Woodford Green
Essex
IG8 7NG

Scalefour Society
1 Eastcote Road
Pinner
Middx
HA5 1DS

Double O Gauge Association
P O Box 100
Crawley
Sussex
RH10 1XP

Gauge O Guild
Membership Secretary
The Old School
Flatts Lane
Wombleton
York
YO6 5RU

As well as these 'scale' societies, you may wish to join the **Historical Model Railway Society**. As described elsewhere in this book, the HMRS is an educational charity set up to provide historical data for railway modellers.

HMRS Membership Secretary
11 Gorse Ave
Mansfield
Notts
NG18 3NS

BIBLIOGRAPHY
Most of the books in the list below cover plastic kit construction and other aspects of modelling in plastic. However, *Simply Scenery* and *Landscape Modelling* are (as their titles suggest) useful as guides to the scenic setting for your Ratio models. *Southern Nouveau* is the standard work on the prototype concrete lineside structures that were prefabricated at the LSWR's Exmouth Junction works. (Ratio produce several of these in model form and Ratio's designers based the kits on the engineers' drawings in *Southern Nouveau*.) Most of the books can either be bought at model railway specialist retailers and exhibitions or ordered through book shops.

Getting the Best from Plastic Wagon Kits
Irwell Press, ISBN 1 871608 56 2

Detailing and Improving RTR Wagons
Irwell Press, ISBN 1 871608 42 2

Painting and Lining in the Smaller Scales
Irwell Press, ISBN 1 871608 55 4

Simply Scenery
Irwell Press, ISBN 1 871608 36 8

Plastic Structure Kits
Wild Swan, ISBN 0 906867 71 1

Landscape Modelling
Wild Swan, ISBN 0 906867 44 4

Southern Nouveau
Wild Swan, ISBN 0 906867 47 9

MAIL ORDER SUPPLIERS
If you do not have a hobby shop or model railway retailer within easy reach, you can buy any of the products mentioned in this book by mail order. The notes below each address give you an idea of each firm's specialities.

Alan Gibson
The Bungalow
Lingwood

Norwich
NR13 4TR
Straight brass wire in several sizes

Cove Models
44 Cove Road
Farnborough
Hants
GU14 0EN
Ratio kits, general modelling supplies, paints, tools, Plastikard

Eileen's Emporium
55 Reedsdale Gardens
Gildersome
Leeds
LS27 7JD
Tools, Fineline Styrene, Plastikard, general modellers supplies

EMA Model Supplies
58—60 The Centre
Feltham
Middlesex
TW13 4BH *Distributors of Fineline Styrene and Plastruct ranges*

Exactoscale Ltd
29 Couchmore Avenue
Esher
Surrey
KT10 9AS
Various architectural detailing components, pre-printed windows

Expo Drills and Tools
10 Bishopric
Horsham
West Sussex
RH12 1QR
Specialist tool suppliers for modelmakers

John K Flack
1 Meadowbank
Kilmington
Axminster
Devon
EX13 7RL
Tools, modelling materials, Evergreen styrene sheet and strip

Freestone Model Accessories
28 Newland Mill
Whitney
Oxfordshire
OX8 6HH
Cutting mats, modellers tools, pre-printed glazing, specialist in card kits

Mainly Trains
13 Anchor Street
Watchet
Somerset
TA23 0AZ
Ratio kits, general modelling supplies, paints, tools, Plastikard

Proops Brothers Limited
24 Saddington Road
Fleckney
Leicester
LE8 8AW
Specialist tool suppliers for modelmakers and jewellers

Shesto
Unit 2
Sapcote Trading Estate
High Street
London NW10 2HD
Specialist tool suppliers for modelmakers and jewellers

Slaters Plastikard
Temple Road
Matlock Bath
Derbyshire
DE4 3PG
Plastikard plain styrene sheet, Plastikard embossed styrene sheet, Microstrip, Microrod

Wills
Lower Road
Forest Hill
Sussex
RH18 5HE
Moulded styrene sheet, architectural accessories, plastic structure kits

APPENDIX 2
ROLLING STOCK KITS

The carriage and wagon kits are all in 4mm scale and Ratio does not plan to produce them in either 2mm or 7mm scales. Some rolling stock kits appear in the photographs in this book. Brief details of the rest (which are all illustrated in the Ratio catalogue) are listed below.

I have not devoted a chapter specifically to Ratio's rolling stock because most of the techniques described in this book apply as much to a wagon as to a building – after all, they are made of the same material and produced by the same process.

Wagon kit construction and modification is dealt with very fully in a sister *Modelling Railways Illustrated Handbook*. Titled *Getting the Best from Plastic Wagon Kits*, it is now in its second reprinting and is available from most good model shops and at many model railway exhibitions. It can also be ordered from book shops or direct from the publishers, Irwell Press, at the address given in Appendix 1.

There have also been many articles about Ratio wagons in the model railway press. So it is always worth browsing through the back issues that are sold cheaply at nearly every model railway exhibition. In particular, look out for the article by John Chambers on Ratio china clay wagons published in *Modelling Railways Illustrated, Volume 1, No. 2* and for Martin Goodall's excellent articles in *Model Railway Journal*.

Some of Ratio's rolling stock kits include metal wheelsets but most come with 00 gauge wheelsets moulded in plastic. These can be easily replaced if you prefer metal wheels. If you model to EM or P4 track and wheel standards, you'll have to replace them anyway. Ratio rolling stock kits readily accommodate alternative wheelsets fitted with standard 26mm pinpoint axles.

You may wish to arrange compensation if you are working to EM or P4 standards. Again, the Ratio models are relatively easy to convert using commercial rocking W irons. This work is fully covered in *Getting the Best from Plastic Wagon Kits*.

Other modifications are equally easy. All Ratio rolling stock kits include a version of the tension-lock coupling in every kit but almost any of the common alternatives (three-link, Alex Jackson, Spratt & Winkle) can be fitted. Cast or turned replacement buffers are available from the ABS, MJT, Kean Maygib and Kenline ranges. There are also numerous brake gear components on the market. Useful books include *Detailing and Improving Ready to Run Wagons* from Irwell Press and the two volumes of Geoff Kent's *The 4mm Wagon*, published by Wild Swan. Details are in Appendix 1.

When it comes to building model carriages, there is rather less published information. Well-known modeller Tony Wright is preparing a *Modelling Railways Illustrated Handbook* (sister to this volume) on the subject and Wild Swan publish the excellent books on carriage modelling by Pendon Museum's Stephen Williams.

CARRIAGE COMPONENTS

One very useful aspect of the Ratio carriage kits is that many of the individual mouldings are available separately. Components include complete bogies, some of the underframes, the roofs, many of the sides and the carriage seating. This product is familiar to many kit builders because several other manufacturers include Ratio's carriage seating in their kits.

Roofs listed by Ratio as stock items are listed below together with a photograph showing their profiles. The roofs are a very useful aid to both kit and scratch builders. There are five types available:

[113] Midland Rly suburban stock roof (sprue includes carriage ends, vents and lamp tops). Length 192mm

[115] Midland Rly clerestory roof (sprue includes clerestory, vents and lamp tops. Length 192mm

[118] LNWR arc roof. Length 201mm

[120] GWR four-wheeled stock roof. Length 114mm

[un-numbered] SR Bogie B van roof. Length 200mm

ROLLING STOCK KIT LIST

This list includes all the rolling stock kits and associated products. The complete kits all include wheels, couplings and transfers. I have not included the grounded carriage and van bodies in this listing. (The square brackets have been omitted for clarity.)

Vans and wagons
017 Harveys Bristol Cream van (pre-printed sides and metal sheet)
541 BR Banana Van (can be converted to other BR and LMS types)
542 BR Clayhood china clay open wagon
562 GWR Bogie bolster A (ex-Taff Vale Rly)
563 GWR Iron Mink A van (early type, can be converted to Gunpowder van)
564 GWR 5-plank open wagon (1930s type, can be converted to other types)
565 GWR 12-ton ventilated van (can be converted to other vans)
566 GWR Mogo end-doored motor car van (limited traffic use)
569 GWR 20-ton 4-wheeled Brake Van (includes six depots on transfers)
571 LMS bogie ore wagon (ex-Caledonian Rly)
572 LMS 12-ton ventilated van (can be converted to several types)
573 LMS 3-plank open wagon
591 SR 12-ton ventilated van (uneven planking, can be converted to represent similar LMS and GWR versions)
593 SR (BR) 12-ton ventilated van (ply sided, can be converted to other types)
594 SR 12-ton ventilated van (even planking, can be converted to Dover ferry van and other types)

Sets
575 Permanent way wagons. Four ex-LNWR wagons; two match trucks and two 3-plank opens (complete with moulded rolled steel joists as load and metal wheels)
576 LMS coal wagons. Two ex-LNWR wagons; one 4-plank open and one 5-plank wagon (with metal wheels)

Underframes and wagon components
560 10ft wheelbase RCH underframe
570 9ft wheelbase underframe
124 10ft wheelbase unfitted underframe
125 Diamond frame wagon bogie with spoked wheels
126 GWR wagon bogie with 3-hole disc wheels
127 Brass buffer heads (four)
128 Ratio couplings (four, with uncoupling ramps)
129 Moulded rolled steel joists for wagon loads

Moulded wheelsets on pinpoint axles
130 12mm diameter spoked wagon wheels (four wheelsets)
131 12mm diameter 3-hole disc wagon wheels (four wheelsets)
132 14mm diameter Mansell pattern carriage wheels (four wheelsets)

Carriage kits
592 SR 28-ton bogie parcels/luggage/utility van (with metal wheels)
610 GWR 4-wheeled all third carriage
612 GWR 4-wheeled composite carriage
613 GWR 4-wheeled brake third composite carriage
710 Midland Rly all third suburban (eight compartment)
711 Midland Rly all first suburban (seven compartment)
713 Midland Rly brake third suburban (six compartment)
714 Midland Rly brake third suburban (four compartment)
720 Midland Rly clerestory non-corridor all third/luggage
722 Midland Rly clerestory non-corridor composite
723 Midland Rly clerestory non-corridor brake third
730 LNWR arc roofed corridor all third
732 LNWR arc roofed corridor composite
733 LNWR arc roofed corridor brake composite
734 LNWR arc roofed corridor brake third

Carriage sets
Set 3 Midland Rly suburban (one each of 710, 711 and 713)
Set 4 Midland Rly clerestory (one each of 720, 722 and 723)
Set 5 LNWR arc roofed (one each of 730, 732 and 734)

Carriage components
104 SR 8ft wheelbase bogies (pair)
105 Midland Rly 48ft carriage underframe, bogies and wheels
106 LNWR 50ft carriage underframe, bogies and wheels

107 Midland Rly 10ft wheelbase bogies and wheels (pair)
108 LNWR 8ft wheelbase bogies and wheels (pair)
110 Roof ventilators and lamp tops
111 Corridor connections
112 Midland Rly suburban carriage sides (pair)*
113 Midland Rly suburban carriage roof with ends and ventilators*
114 Midland Rly clerestory carriage sides (pair)*
115 Midland Rly clerestory carriage roof with ventilators*
116 Midland Rly clerestory carriage ends and partitions*
117 LNWR arc roofed carriage sides (pair)*
118 LNWR arc roofed carriage roof*
119 LNWR arc roofed carriage ends and partitions*
120 GWR 4-wheeled carriage roof*
121 GWR 4-wheeled carriage ends and floor*
122 GWR 4-wheeled carriage underframe*
123 GWR 4-wheeled carriage sides (pair)*
* State reference number of complete kit when ordering to identify type of side, roof or end required.

Ratio's seating can be cut to lengths to fit any carriage. In this photgraph, two sections have been cut to fit a little compartment mock-up; the seat profile is clearly shown. You often find Ratio carriage seating included in coach kits from other manufacturers.

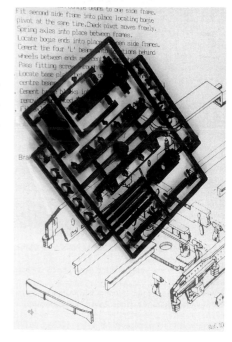

As mentioned in the text, many wagon and coach underframe components are available separately. This is the Southern Railway 8ft steam bogie [104] from the SR Bogie B passenger van kit.

A rake of Ratio wagons built by members of Wolverhampton Model Railway Club. Photo: Tony Wright.

APPENDIX 3
THE BUILDER PACKS RANGE

Ratio's Builder Packs range of architectural surfaces and accessories is only produced in 2mm scale. The range is primarily designed for modellers who wish to scratchbuild architectural structures, but many of the products are very useful when modifying, kitbashing or crosskitting Ratio's 2mm scale models. The Builder Packs components can also be used to add detail to the full kits.

The backbone of the Builder Pack range is the series of moulded styrene sheets representing common architectural surfaces such as brick and stone walling, slates and tiles, and so on. A full list appears below.

Each sheet (most are moulded in pairs on a single sprue) measures 90mm by 75mm. The sheets are just over 1mm thick, which means that strong, rigid structures can be constructed without the need for a sub-shell or extensive internal bracing. Against this advantage, cutting the sheets (particularly for door and window openings) demands some care. The Builder Pack sheets are supplemented by etched brass windows and sprues of moulded styrene detailing components. There are two sets of windows, domestic and industrial. The domestic etch includes casement and sash types, with and without toplights. The industrial set has arched-topped and square framed windows in several configurations and a selection of fanlights.

The detailing components include moulded styrene gutters and downpipes, chimneys, and doors. Several of the mouldings from 2mm scale complete kits also figure in the Builder Pack range, among them the vacuum formed curved corrugated roof, oil tanks and coal staithes.

COMPLEMENTARY PRODUCTS FOR 4mm SCALE

Ratio is not planning to introduce the Builder Pack range in other scales. However, a similar range of products, the Wills Scenic Series, caters to 4mm scale modellers.

The Wills range includes over two dozen moulded sheets, ranges of moulded styrene and metal detailing components and a range of complete Craftsman's Kits.

The 4mm scale Wills sheets are nearly twice as thick – at about two millimetres – as Ratio's 2mm scale sheets. The styrene products in the Wills range are fully compatible with Ratio kits and by combining the two firms' products, a huge range of possibilities is opened up. The Wills products are widely advertised in the model railway press and are stocked in most model railway shops. Fuller details are available from Wills; the address is in Appendix 1.

FURTHER READING

The Wild Swan book *Plastic Structure Kits* is a guide to architectural modelling using moulded styrene components. Although specifically written with the Wills 4mm scale range of products in mind; most of the techniques described in the book are equally effective for the 2mm scale Ratio Builder Pack range. Further details are in the Bibliography in Appendix 1.

BUILDER PACK 2mm SCALE PRODUCT LIST

300 Gutters (two 110mm lengths and two 88mm lengths), straight downpipes (four 35mm lengths) and angled downpipes (four 35mm lengths)
301 Brick walling, common stretcher bond (four 75mm x 90mm mouldings)
302 Coursed coarse stone walling (four 75mm x 90mm mouldings)
303 Crazy paving (four 75mm x 90mm mouldings)
304 Wooden planking (four 75mm x 90mm mouldings)
305 Slate roof (four 75mm x 90mm mouldings)
306 Tile roof (four 75mm x 90mm mouldings)
307 Chimneys (two 2-pot and two single pot chimney stacks as supplied in the station building kit)
308 Pavement flagstones (four 75mm x 90mm mouldings)
309 Industrial windows (brass etching with 28 components)
310 Domestic windows (brass etching with 45 components)
311 Assorted doors (two mouldings with 22 components)
312 Flat corrugated sheet (four 75mm x 90mm mouldings)
313 Rough cast concrete or rendered walling (four 75mm x 90mm mouldings)
314 Industrial brickbuilt chimney stack
315 Oil tanks
316 Coal staithes
317 Curved corrugated roof

APPENDIX 4
GLOSSARY

Adhesive Something used to bond two surfaces together. For styrene, the most common adhesives are liquid organic solvents and viscous cements. For detailing components and other materials, types include contact adhesives, cyanoacrylates, epoxy resin and PVA.

Araldite Brand name of an epoxy resin adhesive (see *Adhesives*).

Architectural surface In modelling terminology, generally used to mean a relief representation of things such as brickwork, cobblestones, roof tiles and so on.

Bargeboard A sloping board on a gable end to protect the end of the roof.

'Big Four' see *Grouping*.

Blind hole One that does not go right through the component it is drilled, or moulded, in.

Bufferbeam see *Underframe*

Cement A clear viscous adhesive for uniting plastic components. Not to be confused with the bonding material between courses of brickwork, referred to as 'mortar' in this book.

Clerestory The raised central part of a railway carriage roof. The term, borrowed from architecture, also describes a carriage so fitted.

Compensation A system to allow the wheelsets of rolling stock to accommodate unevenness in the track. Although not provided for in ratio's rolling stock kits, compensation components can easily be installed in most of them.

Component The individual bits of the kit. (The word 'part' is used as a verb in this book and also refers to the point at which the halves of the mould separate.)

Coupling The device used on model locomotives and rolling stock to couple them together. The most common type (found on British RTR models) is called the tension lock coupling. Ratio supplies its own version (which is compatible with most RTR types) in the rolling stock kits. Less obtrusive types (for instance, scale three link couplings) are easily substituted.

Crosskitting Using components from two or more kits (either from one or more manufacturers) to produce a composite model.

Cyanoacrylate see *Superglue, Adhesives*

Distressing Reproducing the characteristics of age, weathering and wear on a model, usually by marring or exaggerating its surface texture (see also *Weathering*).

Downpipe, downspout A drainpipe on a building, usually vertical, which takes rainwater from a gutter to a drain.

Dry run Temporarily assembling components without bonding them to check their location or fit.

Eaves The overhanging portion at the bottom of a roof.

EM see *Gauge*

Epoxy resin A type of adhesive in two gel components must be mixed together to effect hardening (see *Adhesives*).

Etching As a verb, it describes the photochemical process of forming small components from thin sheet metal. As a noun, 'etching' refers to an individual component on the sheet (as in 'attach the etching with epoxy adhesive').

Extraction The process by which the moulding is automatically ejected from the mould tool. The process is aided by tapering and by moulded-on extraction pips (see *Pips* and *Release taper*).

Feed The thin web of plastic which joins the component to the runner, usually the best place to cut when removing components.

Flashing A sealing strip of lead or fillet of cement used to keep water out where chimneys or dormers project from a roof. On a model, flashing can be represented by filler and used to disguise joints.

Flaunching The mortar seal between a chimney stack and the individual pots.

Filler Any material used to fill unwanted gaps between assembled components or remedy surface blemishes. Fillers are usually in the form of a pliable paste which hardens after application.

Finial On a building, a finial is architectural ornament at the apex of a gable end. On a signal, it is the shaped 'spike' at the top of the post.

Flash The unwanted irregular wafer-thin protrusion along the part-line of the component. It is formed if a little molten plastic seeps between two faces of the mould tool.

Foliage mat An open textured, fibrous material with ground foam or scenic scatter embedded in it.

Fret A sheet of etched metal, including the framework and the individual items (as in 'do not remove components from the fret until you need them').

Gable end The end of a building where the roof slopes meet.

Gauge The distance between the inside faces of the two rails of track. There are various track gauges used in each modelling scale. Confusion arises because scale and gauge are often used rather loosely.

0 gauge (that's 0 as in zero, not as in Oscar) can safely be used as a synonym for 7mm scale. The most common track gauge is 32mm which is slightly under scale; 33mm is more accurate and is the gauge adopted for S7.

In 4mm scale, things are slightly more confusing. The most commonly used track gauge is 16.5mm – this is called 00 gauge (note that 00 is not a scale). However, 16.5mm is considerably under scale in 4mm:1ft. EM gauge (the letters stand for eighteen millimetres) is still under scale but a lot closer than 00. P4 track and wheel standards are virtually true to scale and the track gauge is 18.83mm.

So any Ratio 4mm scale model (except, obviously, the wheels supplied with the rolling stock kits) can be used on layouts whether they have 00, EM or P4 track. However, 4mm scale models will be considerably over scale on H0 layouts, where the scale is 3.5mm:1ft (see *HO*).

In 2mm:1ft scale things are also not quite as straightforward as they seem either. British N (the N stands for nine) uses a track gauge of 9mm but the scale is 2.062mm:1ft; therefore the track gauge is considerably underscale. In the rest of the world, N means 2mm:1ft scale on 9mm gauge track; the track gauge is still a bit under scale. In Britain, modellers of true scale 2mm:1ft use a track gauge of 9.42mm. In practice, Ratio 2mm scale models can be used for any N or 2mm scale layout.

Glazing The representation of 'glass' in model windows. For larger areas, it is usually clear styrene sheet such as Slaters Plastiglaz. For very small areas (such as the spectacle glasses of signal arms, liquid glazing such as Carr's Window Glaze is better.

Glazing bars The components of a window frame that support the panes of glass.

Grouping In 1923, the multitude of independent railway companies were amalgamated into four groups ('often referred to as the 'Big Four'). These were the Great Western Railway (GWR), the London, Midland and Scottish Railway (LMS), the London North Eastern Railway (LNER) and the Southern Railway (SR). In 1948, all four were combined into the nationalised British Railways (BR).

Therefore, the term pre-grouping means prior to 1923 and post grouping means after 1948.

Headstock The cross member that carries the buffers on a carriage or wagon. It's only called a bufferbeam or bufferplank on a locomotive (see also *Underframe*).

HO *Not* the same as 00. H0 models are to a scale of 3.5mm:1ft. In H0, the track gauge of 16.5mm is virtually to scale (see also *Gauge*).

Infrastructure All the fixed and permanent parts of the railway system such as track, electrification equipment, signalling, bridges, stations and so on.

Kitbashing Using or modifying the components of a kit to produce a different model than the manufacture intended.

Livery The standard scheme of painting, lining and lettering applied to the locomotives and rolling stock of a particular railway company or train operator. Sometimes extended to mean the corporate colours used on the infrastructure.

Louvre An arrangement of overlapping angled boards, planks or slats to allow ventilation but exclude rain, for example the roof vent on the Ratio engine shed.

Loading gauge, a In order to ensure that loads placed on wagons or other railways vehicles would not foul structures such as bridges, a fixed height gauge was used. These were most often found where sidings, goods depots, marshalling yards and so on were connected to running lines.

Loading gauge, the Loosely, a set of fixed dimensions to govern the relationship between rolling stock and lineside structures.

Microrod Thin round-section styrene 'wire' manufactured by several firms. The Slaters variety (listed as Plastic Rod) is available in diameters from 10thou to 50thou (0.25mm to 1.25mm).

Microstrip Lengths of small rectangular section styrene manufactured by several firms, notably Slaters. Microstrip comes in a wide variety of width/thickness combinations, ranging from 10thou x 20thou (approx 0.25mm x 0.5mm) to 276thou x 60thou (approx 7mm x 1.5mm).

Mortar see *Cement*

Moulding As a verb, the process of forming plastic to shape. As a noun, the resulting individual piece.

Mould tool The pair of steel plates from which the shape of the desired component has been cut and into which the molten plastic is injected.

N Gauge see *Gauge*

0 see *Gauge*

00 see *Gauge*

Organic solvent see *Adhesives*

P4 see *Gauge*

Paling Wooden fencing consisting of vertical or, less frequently, sloping parallel narrow boards attached to horizontal rails. The individual boards are called pales.

Pare To cut material from a component little by little using a slicing action.

Part-line Mould tools come in two halves and, because it is virtually impossible to align them absolutely perfectly, a line or step appears around the finished moulding where they meet, particularly with round components.

Pip Small projections moulded onto the component, usually on the back, the inside or along an edge. Some pips are intended to help the modeller locate components during assembly but most are to facilitate extraction from the mould. These usually need removing.

Plastiglaz see *Glazing*

Plastikard Brand name for a Slaters product (but 'plasticard' has become a generic term for smooth styrene sheet), the basic material used for modelling in plastic and for detailing or kitbashing Ratio models. Styrene sheet embossed or moulded to represent various architectural surfaces is also available.

Polystyrene Usually abbreviated to styrene, it is the hard plastic in which Ratio kits are moulded. Most other plastic kits and many RTR models are made of styrene.

Prototype In modelling parlance, this refers to the real, full sized, item being modelled rather than the first of something.

PVA A thick, creamy adhesive used in woodwork. It can be diluted with water, dries clear and has many uses in model railway construction.

Quadrant, upper and lower A semaphore signal arm which is horizontal is at danger. If it rises (usually by about 30°) to clear, it is termed an upper quadrant signal; if it falls to clear, it is a lower quadrant (see also *Signal terminology*).

Release taper To facilitate extraction from the mould, some components have to be moulded with an otherwise-unwanted slight taper.

Ridge The point at which the two slopes of a roof meet.

RTR Used in this book as an abbreviation of 'ready to run'.

Rolling stock Railway vehicles except locomotives. Passenger vehicles are often described as coaches although the railway term is carriage. Open goods vehicles are generally called wagons and roofed ones vans.

Runner This is the short section of plastic which unites the component to the sprue.

Scale The relationship of a model to its prototype; 4mm:1ft (4mm scale) means that four millimetres on the model represents one foot on the real thing. Ratio produce models in 2mm, 4mm and 7mm scales.

Scale is not the same as gauge but the two terms are often used synonymously. 'Non-railway' items (by which I mean most models on a layout other than the trackwork and rolling stock) intended for 2mm scale layouts are often described as 'N Gauge'; those for 4mm scale as '00 Gauge' or (confusinfly) as '00/H0 Gauge' and those for 7mm scale as '0 Gauge'.

Scenic scatter Granular or powder materials in 'natural' colours which are used to produce the effect of earth, grass, foliage and so on.

Scrape To draw the knife bladeor scalpel edge-on

along the a component to smooth or reduce it.

Signal terminology A 'stop' signal is just that – a signal at which trains must stop if it's at danger. The arm, square-ended, is red with a white band. Many modellers incorrectly refer to all such signals as 'home' signals. A stop signal may be a home signal but it often isn't.

A 'distant' signal gives advance warning of whether the next stop signal is at danger or is clear. Therefore a train may usually pass a distant signal which is at danger. The arm, with a fish-tail end, is usually yellow with a black chevron band.

A signal at danger is often said to be 'on'. When it clear, it is said to be 'off'.

Refer to the diagram in Chapter 7 for the names of individual signal components.

Solvent In plastic kit construction, solvents are liquids used to bond styrene (see also *Adhesives*). In painting, solvents (often referred to as thinners) are liquids used to dilute paint, remove residues and to clean equipment.

Spectacle see *Signal terminology*

Sprue The framework of plastic which supports the individual components on a moulding. The term is sometimes used to describe the whole moulding.

Steam age Used in this book to encompass the period from the turn of the century to the early 1970s. (Although steam traction vanished from many parts of British Railways during the early 1960s and finished entirely in mid-1968, it was several years before the operation and appearance of the railway changed dramatically.)

Styrene see *Polystyrene*

Sheet see *Plastikard*

Sub-assembly Components built up into a unit, several of which will be united in the completed model.

Superglue The common name for cyanoacrylate adhesives (see *Adhesives*)

Taper see *Release*

Test assembly The same as a dry run.

Thinner A solvent used to dilute paint or clean brushes and equipment.

Thou No, not the archaic singular pronoun of the second person. It's simply an abbreviation of one thousandth of an inch which is the commonly used unit of measurement for the thickness sheet materials. Forty thou equals one millimetre.

Underframe The framework of a carriage or wagon which carries the wheels or bogies and on which the vehicle's body is built up. A prototype underframe is a complicated structure with a lot of cross bracing; on the model the visible parts are the solebars (the longitudinal outside members which, on a wagon or van, carry the W irons and axleboxes) and the headstocks (the correct name for the transverse outside end members which carry the buffers and coupling). Ratio supplies underframes from the complete kits as separate items.

Vacuum forming An alternative method of producing components from styrene (see also *Moulding*).

Wet'n'dry A convenient colloquialism for the tough waterproof carbide abrasive paper used in the automotive finishing industry. It is the most useful product for rubbing down models.

The term generally used to indicate its degree of abrasiveness is 'grit'. For modelling, 120 grit paper is coarse, 240 grit medium and 400 grit fine. 600 grit and above is rather too fine for use with styrene; it can only used to burnish away fine scratches.

Weathering The appearance and condition of most prototypes structures is affected by weather and pollution. Reproducing this in model form by dulling surfaces, using soft or faded colours, painting to represent dirt and so on is called weathering (see also *Distressing*).

Wheelset A pair of wheels mounted on an axle.

APPENDIX 5
COMPLETE LISTS OF RATIO PRODUCTS

The following lists include all Ratio's kits and associated products together with recommended retail prices. The lists were complete (and the prices correct) at the time of writing, January 1996.

Inevitably, some prices may change during this book's currency. Please write to Ratio for the latest price list, enclosing a large stamped self-addressed envelope.

Most of these kits are available through hobby shops and specialist model railway retailerss. If you do not have a retailer near you, refer to Appendix 1.

If you order direct from Ratio, remember that orders of £10.00 and over are post free but packing and postage on orders under £10.00 costs £1.

All Ratio products (including individual mouldings from the kits) are available to personal callers at Ratio's factory shop. The factory is located near the centre of Buckfastleigh and is open during normal business hours from Monday to Thursday and on Friday mornings. It is always advisable to telephone first to confirm opening and to get directions from the town centre.

List one: 2mm scale lineside items
202 Cattle dock £8.75
203 Engine shed (single road) £7.25
204 Station building £11.25
205 Station building canopy £1.75
206 Locomotive servicing depot £8.75
208 Apex platform canopy £4.50
209 Platform £2.30
210 Platform ramps £2.30
211 Telegraph poles £2.00
213 Station lamp posts £2.30
214 Yard crane £2.30
215 Square water tower with two water cranes £4.50
216 Post-and-rail three-bar lineside fencing (white) £2.00
217 As 216 (brown) £2.00
218 Signal ladder (etched brass) £2.30
219 Concrete panel fencing (with gates) £2.00
220 Goods shed £7.25
221 Pallets, sacks and barrels £1.75
222 Concrete footbridge £4.50
223 GWR Signal box (with interior) £7.25
224 Signal box interior and window frames (etched brass)£2.95
225 Flat platform canopy with valance £4.50
226 Pump or boiler house £7.25
227 Weighbridge with hut £3.50
228 Oil depot £3.50
229 Coal depot £3.50
230 Cylindrical water tower £3.50
231 Carriage shed £7.50
232 Builders' merchant £6.25
233 Loading gauge £2.30
234 Gated level crossing £4.50
235 Barrier level crossing £4.50
236 Midland Rly signal box (no interior) £6.95
237 Two huts (one brick, one wood) £2.95

List two: 2mm signals and accessories
249 Diesel/electric locomotive headlamps (four per pack)£1.50
250 Remote control apparatus £1.75
260 Lower quadrant (with stop and distant arms) £1.50
262 Lower quadrant bracket (with stop and distant arms) £2.75
263 Four ground signalsPOA
270 Upper quadrant (with stop and distant arms) £1.50
271 Pratt truss gantry £1.75

List three: 2mm Builder Pack range
300 Gutters £2.30
301 Brick walling £2.30
302 Coursed coarse stone walling £2.30
303 Crazy paving £2.30
304 Wooden planking £2.30
305 Slate roof £2.30
306 Tile roof £2.30
307 Chimneys £2.30
308 Pavement flagstones £2.30
309 Industrial windows £2.30
310 Domestic windows £2.30
311 Assorted doors £2.30
312 Flat corrugated sheet £2.30
313 Rough cast concrete walling £2.30
314 Industrial chimney £2.45
315 Oil tanks £2.30
316 Coal staithes £2.30
317 Curved corrugated roof £1.75

List four: 4mm scale lineside items
411 GWR/LMS loading gauge £1.75
419 Concrete fence posts with gates £2.95
420 Paling fencing with ramped sections and gates (white) £2.30
421 Paling fencing (white) £1.75
422 Paling fencing (black) £1.75
423 Concrete post post-and-wire fencing £1.75
424 Post-and-rail fencing, four bar (white) £1.75
425 Post-and-rail fencing, four bar (black) £1.75
426 Midland Rly slanted paling fencing (white) £1.75
427 Midland Rly slanted paling fencing (black) £1.75
429 Concrete panel fencing £2.30
430 Palling fence (as 420, but green) £2.30
431 Paling fencing (as 421, but green) £1.75
434 GWR style metal spear fencing £2.30
451 Signal ladders (four lengths) £1.75
452 Telegraph poles £2.30
453 Swan-necked lamp posts £2.30
454 Concrete lamp posts £2.50

List five: 4mm scale lineside buildings and structures
500 GWR Signal box £9.25
501 Grounded carriage body (short) £3.25
502 Cattle dock £9.75
503 Platform level GWR signal box (similar to kit 500) £9.25
504 Station building £15.95
505 Coaling stage £4.50
506 Square water tower £9.25
507 Grounded van body £2.75
508 Pump or boiler house £9.25
509 Occupation crossing £2.75
510 Industrial chimney (cylindrical 'metal' type) £1.75
511 Pair of lineside huts £2.75
512 Skylights (can be used as garden coldframes) £1.75
513 Concrete prefabricated traders' store £9.25
514 Pallets, sacks and oil drums £1.75
515 Apex platform canopy with valances £7.75
516 Canopy valances and notice boards £1.75
517 Concrete footbridge £6.75
518 Pair of concrete lineside huts £3.10
519 Grounded carriage body (long) £4.50
520 Station platform £4.50
521 Assorted brick arches suitable for industrial buildings£1.20
522 Engine shed (single road) £14.75
523 Arched industrial multi-paned window frames £1.75
524 Weighbridge with hut £2.95
525 Coal or builders' merchant £11.75
526 Filled sacks (48) £2.30
527 Carriage shed £11.75
528 GWR conical water tower (can be built with flat top)£6.75
529 Oil distribution depot £7.75
530 Pair of tanks from kit 529 £4.50
531 Yard crane £5.95
532 Coal depot £4.95
533 Coal staithes £2.75
534 Goods shed £15.95
535 Brickbuilt hut or yard office £2.00
536 Midland Rly signal box £12.50
537 Retaining wall £3.95
538 Gutters and down pipes £2.50
539 MR signal box windows £2.50

List six: 4mm scale signals
460 GWR square post stop signal £5.50
461 GWR square post distant signal £5.50
462 GWR square post stop signal with lower arm distant£6.95
469 GWR square post bracket signal £5.95
470 LMS tubular post stop signal £5.50
471 LMS tubular post distant signal £5.50
490 SR railbuilt post stop signal £5.50
491 SR railbuilt post distant signal £5.50
492 SR railbuilt post stop signal with lower arm distant£6.95
465 Ground signals (four) £1.95
466 GWR square post signals £4.50
467 GWR tubular post signals £1.75
476 LMS tubular post signals £4.50
477 LNWR square post signals £4.50
478 Pratt truss gantry £1.75
486 LNER lattice post signals £4.50
134 Signal levers (pair) £1.60
135 4mm scale cord control system £1.60
136 Cord control extension pack £0.85
137 Signal arms with lenses, long and short types £0.85
138 Point control (for Peco type operation) £1.75*
139 Signal box windows £0.85
140 Signal box chimneys £0.85
142 Signal box stair case £0.60

List seven: 4mm scale rolling stock kits
017 Pre-printed Harveys Bristol Cream van £3.95
541 BR banana van £3.50
542 China clay wagon £3.19
560 Wagon underframe, 10ft wheelbase £1.75
562 GWR bogie bolster wagon £3.50
563 GWR Iron Mink van £3.50
564 GWR 5-plank open wagon £3.50
565 GWR 12-ton ventilated van £3.50
566 GWR Mogo van £3.50
569 GWR 20-ton Toad brake van £3.50
570 Wagon underframe, 9ft wheelbase £1.75
571 LMS bogie ore wagon £3.50
572 LMS 12-ton ventilated van £3.50
573 LMS 3-plank open wagon £3.50
575 Four ex-LNWR permanent way wagons £12.75
576 Two ex-LNWR coal wagons £6.75
591 SR 12-ton 'uneven plank' ventilated van £3.50
592 SR Bogie passenger van £12.95
593 SR 12-ton 'ply' ventilated van £3.50
594 SR 12-ton 'even plank' ventilated van £3.50
610 GWR 4-wheeled all third carriage £4.95
612 GWR 4-wheeled composite carriage £4.95
613 GWR 4-wheeled brake third composite carriage £4.95
710 Midland Rly all third suburban (eight compartment) £8.25
711 Midland Rly all first suburban (seven compartment) £8.25
713 Midland Rly brake third suburban (six compartment) £8.25
714 Midland Rly brake third suburban (four compartment) £8.25
720 Midland Rly clerestory non-corridor all third/luggage £8.25
722 Midland Rly clerestory non-corridor composite £8.25
723 Midland Rly clerestory non-corridor brake third £8.25
730 LNWR arc roofed corridor all third £9.95*
732 LNWR arc roofed corridor composite £9.95*
733 LNWR arc roofed corridor brake composite £9.95*
734 LNWR arc roofed corridor brake third £9.95*
433 Carriage seating £1.75

Carriage Gift Sets
Set 3 MR suburban (one each of 710, 711 and 713) £22.50
Set 4 MR clerestory (one each of 720, 722 and 723) £22.50
Set 5 LNWR arc roofed (one each of 730, 732 and 734) £27.50*

List eight: 7mm scale kits
071 GWR square post signal (specify stop or distant) £9.95
072 Signal ladder £1.95
073 Telegraph poles £2.95
074 Concrete panel fencing £4.50
* Limited availability

List nine: ex-factory items, individual components and accessories
The following products are not generally available through the model trade. They can be purchased from Ratio by mail order, from the firm's sales stand at model railway exhibitions or by a visit to the Buckfastleigh factory. General enquiries should be accompanied by a stamped self-addressed envelope. For orders under £10.00, please add £1 to cover packing and postage. Orders of £10.00 and over are post free

Note that liquid products - Polsol adhesive, Modoil and track cleaning fluid - **are not** supplied by post and can only be purchased at exhibitions or by visitors to the factory.

As well as the products listed here, Ratio can supply any complete individual moulding from any of the kits. The whole range (subject to stockholding) is available to factory visitors. For mail order supply, write to Ratio for a quotation, describing the component or moulding you require and identifying which kit it is part of. All enquiries about individual mouldings **must** be accompanied by a stamped, self-addressed envelope.

Individual mouldings are also available from the Ratio sales stand at model railway exhibitions - however, with over a thousand mouldings to choose from, only a limited selection can be offered at any one exhibition.

104 SR 8ft wheelbase bogies (pair) £2.50
105 MR 48ft carriage underframe, bogies and wheels £4.95
106 LNWR 50ft carriage underframe, bogies and wheels £4.95
107 MR 10ft wheelbase bogies (pair) and wheels £2.50
108 LNWR 8ft wheelbase bogies (pair) and wheels £2.50
110 Roof ventilators and lamp tops £0.85
111 Corridor connections £0.85
112 MR suburban carriage sides (pair) £1.75
113 Roof, ends, ventilators for 112 £1.75
114 MR clerestory carriage sides (pair) £1.75
115 Roof and ventilators for 114 £1.75
116 Ends and partitions for 114 £1.75
117 LNWR arc roofed carriage sides (pair) £1.75
118 Roof for 117 £1.75
119 Ends and partitions for 117 £1.75
120 GWR 4-wheeled carriage roof£1.25
121 GWR 4-wheeled carriage ends and floor £1.25
122 GWR 4-wheeled carriage underframe £1.25
123 GWR 4-wheeled carriage sides (pair) £1.25

When ordering roofs and ends (items 112-123 above), please include the reference number of the complete kit (see List seven, above) to identify the specific type of side or end required.

124 10ft wheelbase unfitted underframe £1.75
125 Diamond frame wagon bogie with spoked wheels £1.75
126 GWR wagon bogie with 3-hole disc wheels £1.75
127 Brass buffer heads (four) £0.85
128 Ratio couplings (four, with uncoupling ramps) £1.30
129 Moulded rolled steel joists for wagon loads £1.30
130 12mm diameter spoked wagon wheels (four axles) £0.55
131 12mm diameter disc wagon wheels (four axles) £0.55
132 14mm diameter Mansell carriage wheels (four axles) £0.55

Bulk packs of item 138 (point control for Peco type operation)
Pack of seven units £11.50
Pack of fourteen units £22.00

Polsol liquid plastic adhesive £1.45
Modoil £1.15
Track cleaning fluid (small) £0.85
Track cleaning fluid (large) £1.15